Highways
of the South
Landmarks and Legacies

Stephen H. Provost

All material © 2021 Stephen H. Provost
Cover concept and design: Stephen H. Provost
Cover photograph: Stephen H. Provost
Back cover: Stephen H. Provost
All contemporary photographs © 2018-2021 Stephen H. Provost
Historical images are in the public domain, except where noted

No part of this book may be reproduced, or stored in a retrieval system, or transmitted in any form or by any means, electronic, mechanical, photocopying, recording, or otherwise, without the express written permission of the publisher.

Dragon Crown Books 2021

All rights reserved.

ISBN 978-1-949971-18-7

Dedication

To all who value history and recognize the importance of preserving it.

Contents

Introduction   7

Part I: Southern Connections
Trails to Turnpikes   13
Down on Main Street   49
Highway to Heaven   73
Road to Perdition   91
Pride and Prejudice   111

Part II: Southern Comforts
Full Tank, Will Travel   129
Are We There Yet?   149
Delightful Diversions   171
All the Fixin's   197
Plum Tuckered Out   235
Made You Look!   273

Front cover photo by Stephen H. Provost:
    Star Light Motel, Mt. Airy, N.C., 2019 (adapted)

Back cover photos by Stephen H. Provost:
    Horseshoe Camp, Bowling Green, Ky., 2021 (main)
    Giant Chicken, Marietta, Ga., 2021
    Shell service station, Winston-Salem, N.C., 2019

Volume III
America's Historic Highways

A rural highway near the Virginia-North Carolina state line. *Author photo*

STEPHEN H. PROVOST

More Reading

The America's Historic Highways series

The California's Historic Highways series

Heading east toward Tennessee along U.S. 11 through Abingdon, Va., 2020. *Author photo*

Introduction

Our highways are a microcosm of American life itself, and nowhere is that truer than in the South. A trip down the highway is like a trip through a time capsule, or down the proverbial "Memory Lane." You might pass by a garage from the early 1920s, a service from the station from the 1930s that's been converted into a yogurt shop, a drive-in theater built in the '50s and a fast-food restaurant that went up in the '70s.

Some things change along the highway, and others stay the same. You can still find old taverns and courthouses from the 19th and even the 18th century, and stretches of abandoned concrete or bridges alongside newer roads.

You'll find things in the South you won't find anywhere else, like Krystal burger joints.

And you'll find a host of roadside traditions that started out in the South and were so popular they spread nationwide: Chick-fil-A, Krispy Kreme, Cracker Barrel, and KFC, just to name a few.

No matter where you live, you owe more to the South than you probably realize, from the food you eat to the expressions you use.

But just what is the South?

It might seem easy to define. Take some down-home cookin', toss in some NASCAR, bluegrass and blues (without the grass), and you've got a good idea what a lot of people probably picture when they think of the South — at least people who aren't from the South.

I moved to the region in middle age, having spent most of my life in California. I knew about the Kentucky Derby and Graceland and SEC football, but I couldn't have guessed at the diversity of beauty and culture that awaited me. None of the stereotypes could even begin to do it justice. Some of them were distorted caricatures, and others were just plain off-base.

But the South is a complicated place, just like the highways that crisscross it.

Viewing the South as somehow monolithic is to do it a great disservice. There are great metropolitan centers like Atlanta and Miami; Dallas, New Orleans, and Charlotte, each of them as different from one another as they are from the rural landscape that surrounds them.

There's a sense outside this place that the people here all speak with the same "Southern drawl." But the dialect of Charleston, South Carolina, is as distinct from that of the Ozarks as a Bostonian's accent is from a New Yorker's. New Orleans and Shreveport are both in Louisiana — although you might not know it from hearing them speak; the same goes for the different dialects in Asheville and Raleigh, North Carolina.

The food's a smorgasbord, too. The biscuits really are better in the South, and you'll even find a chain of fast-food eateries called Biscuitville in Virginia and North Carolina. There's no shortage of fried chicken, either. But you'd be kidding yourself if you thought Southern cooking could be summed up on the menu you get at Cracker Barrel. Different crops and different cultures blend to form tantalizing tastes, from the Cajun and Creole cuisine of New Orleans to Texas beef barbecue, to pulled pork and soft shellfish in Virginia.

Even the region itself is hard to define.

HIGHWAYS OF THE SOUTH

According to the Census Bureau, the South consists of everything from Maryland, Delaware, and West Virginia down through Florida, and westward to Texas. But it doesn't include Missouri, even though West Virginia's farther north than the Show-Me State. And despite all this, a poll in 2016 found that most people didn't think Maryland, D.C., or Delaware were in the South. In fact, almost twice as many considered Missouri a Southern state as thought about Maryland that way.

Some people don't think Florida's in the South, even though it's as far south as you can get on the East Coast. Too many snowbirds from NYC for it to qualify. And Texas is its own thing. Don't try to put it into some bigger category.

Confused yet? Now consider that the old Confederacy — which some still use to define the South — didn't include Maryland or Delaware but did control a portion of Arizona. It claimed Kentucky and Missouri, but never actually controlled either state.

For the purposes of this book, I decided to throw a fairly broad net across the South, roughly similar to that used by the Census Bureau, plus Missouri. That is, obviously, a huge swath of territory, and it would be impossible for a single volume to contain all the noteworthy sights and stories that have made the Southern highways what they are. What I've included here is a sampling of what I've come across in my travels and my research. It's meant to represent a cross-section of life on the highway as it was and as it is today, a compendium of the vast and richly diverse history behind these familiar and iconic roads.

Part One
Southern Connections

Country Roads

Dirt section of the Lee Highway, later U.S. 11, in Virginia, 1920. *Library of Congress*

Trails to Turnpikes

Just what is a highway, anyway? In the 21st century, it's easy to think of highways in terms of *interstate* highways — those six- or eight- or more-lane rivers of asphalt that allow us to slice through cityscape and countryside alike with the ease of that proverbial hot knife through butter. Unless, of course, it's rush hour. Or there's an accident. Or there's road construction ahead.

But "highway" is really just another word for "main direct road." At least, that's how Merriam-Webster defines it, and if we take that definition as a starting point, we soon discover it can apply to all manner of roadways: wide and narrow, smooth and bumpy. In fact, the word "highway" long predates the advent of the interstate system, with its blue-and-red shields, created by President Dwight Eisenhower in the mid-1950s. Paved roads date back decades earlier, and dirt, gravel, and macadam roads decades before that. Many of them were called highways, too, and kept right on being called highways after the interstates were built.

Dirt roads once were called highways, and later, concrete or macadam roads with barely room for two cars to pass abreast. Some of these were upgraded, others abandoned, and still others were still called highways, even as they remained in close to their original state.

The first federal highway system, which came into being in 1926, still exists, marked by black lettering on white shields. Some of these roads have been replaced by, or run parallel to, the interstates that provide access to towns and cities along the way via smoothly arcing or cloverleaf on- and off-ramps. Some of the federal highways have those, too, but others don't: On some, you still have to wait at stoplights along the way.

In places, the federal highways might be six lanes wide. In others, they're two-lane country roads that you wouldn't be able to distinguish from state or county byways if it weren't for those shields. The main difference is who pays to maintain them.

With all this in mind, perhaps the best way to define a highway is a main road linking two or more important points (usually towns or cities) a fair distance apart. That leaves out a road from the city center that ends in a rural neighborhood, an industrial site, or a specific attraction.

Early Highways

Some of the nation's oldest highways ran through the South. The King's Highway, built between 1650 and 1750, started out as a trail that ran 1,300 miles from Boston to Charleston, South Carolina. The "king" in question was King Charles II of England, for whom Charleston was named and who instructed his governors to build a road connecting the colonies. It would pass through New York; Philadelphia; Baltimore; Norfolk, Virginia; and Wilmington, North Carolina along the way.

Some of those cities hadn't even been founded yet when construction on the road began. New York was called New Amsterdam, and Charleston was Charles Town. It survives as the basis for sections of several modern roads, including Interstate 95 from Boston to New York, which follows the old Boston Post Road; U.S. 206 and State Route 27 in New Jersey; and U.S. 13 (Frankford Avenue) in northeast Philly. There it crosses the oldest bridge in America. Called variously the Pennypack Creek Bridge, Frankford Avenue Bridge, and King's Highway Bridge, the three-arch stone span was built in 1697.

The Pennypack Creek Bridge in Philadelphia was built in 1697. *Library of Congress*

It enters the South along U.S. 40 from Philadelphia to Alexandria, Virginia, where it was also called the Potomac Trail. There it follows State Highways 1 and 721 as it heads toward North Carolina, where it survives in portions of U.S. Highway 58, State Route 32, and U.S. 17. It endures in a number of communities on street signs that carry names like King Street, King's Road, or King Avenue.

In other places, it's less conspicuous. The last unpaved stretch still accessible to the public is a dirt road on the edge of McClellanville, South Carolina. The Old Georgetown Road, as it's known, is nothing more than a shady lane. A small granite obelisk can still be seen there across from a plot of land once occupied by Jones Tavern, also known as the 32-

Mile House, four miles from town and 32 miles from Charleston (hence the tavern's name). Another old section could be seen running parallel to U.S. 1 in Woodbridge, Virginia.

These stretches of the old road offer a glimpse of what the word "highway" meant in the South during those early years. The *South Carolina Encyclopedia* declared that "even at its best, the condition of the route was seldom good," adding that "narrow roads, ruts, mud, obstructions, and poorly maintained bridges and ferries were just a few of the inconveniences to be expected.

Indeed, "the section between Wilmington and Charleston was judged by some travelers to be 'the most tedious and disagreeable of any on the Continent.'"

The Old Georgetown Road, like many colonial roads, followed an even

Section of the King's Highway along U.S. Highway 1 in Woodbridge, Va. *Library of Congress*

earlier path carved out by Native Americans — in this case, it was known as the Sewee Broad Path. That early road was named for the Sewee tribe, whose territory encompassed a 30-mile strip of land along the Santee River, extending inland from the coast just north of McClellanville.

Other roads branched off the King's Highway and ran parallel to it farther inland. The Great Valley Road forked away westward at Philadelphia, then headed down through Virginia's Shenandoah Valley and southwest to Knoxville, Tennessee. (A second branch continued due south from Roanoke to Charlotte.)

This highway, which also ran along an old Native American trail, later became a privately funded turnpike, or toll road: a key commercial artery that allowed merchants to transport their goods inland from the coast — for a price. You had to stop at a turnstile every five miles to pay a toll, and a 93-mile trip of from one end to the other in 1840 would cost you $100 in today's dollars.

Federal Fallout

Toll roads like the Valley Pike came about because the federal government had pulled back on any involvement in road-building. Legislation in 1806 had set aside federal funds to pay for a road from Cumberland, Maryland, to Ohio, called either the National Road or Cumberland Road, and a proposal was made for an entire network of roads, but this languished over the question of whether the states or the federal government should pay for it.

In 1830, Congress considered a bill to establish roads from Washington, D.C., to Buffalo and New Orleans. The latter road would have passed through Virginia, Tennessee, Alabama, and Mississippi, to Louisiana.

The legislation, however, was defeated in the House on a vote of 105-88 — largely because of opposition in the South. Four congressmen from Tennessee supported it, but otherwise, just one member each from Alabama, Louisiana, and Virginia voted in favor of it. Taken together, the Carolinas, Georgia, and Virginia tipped the balance torpedoing the bill, opposing it by an 34-1 vote.

The irony is that the South would wind up with some of the worst roads going forward into the 20th century.

But the same regional rivalries that fueled distrust in the South toward other regions in the Antebellum period were at the root of the fight over the bill. States' rights were a key point of contention. Virginia Rep. Philip Barbour suggested the bill would benefit western states at the expense of the South, a concern echoed by Tennessee Rep. James K. Polk (later the 11th president), who warned that stronger regions would "overshadow and overpower the weak."

Barbour also said it would be a waste of money, since its value would be "outstripped by railroads" and its $11 million cost would delay repayment of the national debt. And fellow Virginian William Archer argued that the bill would result in rampant corruption.

When it ultimately failed, a *Raleigh Star* editorial was "gratified to learn" of its fate. "Had it been passed into law," the newspaper wrote, it "would at once have sanctioned a doctrine destructive to the rights of the sovereign States of this Union... and extorted from the people the enormous sum of fifteen or twenty [million] dollars, for the construction of a road which, after it was finished, would be of no practical use, except to a few individuals living near its two ends."

It was a huge blow to the concept of federal funding for the nation's roads, but not the final nail in the coffin for the 19th century. That came a month later, when Congress actually passed a more modest bill, dedicating federal funds to buy stock in a private company that sought to build a 66-mile turnpike along the Ohio River in Kentucky.

But Andrew Jackson — a Southerner himself — vetoed it for one of the same reasons Rep. Barbour had opposed the Washington National Road Bill earlier: It would delay repaying the national debt.

The turnpikes wouldn't be getting any federal money, although states did invest in them.

In Tennessee, lawmakers passed a law authorizing the state to pay one-third of the cost, up to $4 million, to build any rail line or highway linking Nashville with Gallatin, about 30 miles away. The Nashville to Gallatin Turnpike Company was formed in response, and another company quickly asked for, and was granted, a charter for a pike from Nashville to Franklin, 22 miles to the north. Before long, more than 900 turnpike companies were operating in the state, and Tennessee stopped granting aid to private roadbuilders in 1840.

The state of Virginia, meanwhile, bought 40 percent of the stock made available by the Valley Turnpike Company, which sold $250,000 of stock to pay for the project along the Great Valley Road: 10,000 shares at $25 apiece. The road was a thoroughly modern "macadamized" route, which meant it was upgraded using recently developed method of paving with three layers of crushed rock. It also had drainage ditches.

(Not all turnpikes were macadamized. In swampy areas, plank and corduroy — log — roads were laid down in some places. In the South, plank roads were particularly popular in North Carolina, which had 54 of them, but the vast majority were in the Northeast and Midwest.)

The Valley Turnpike was heavily damaged by troop movements during the Civil War, and the advent of the railroad reduced its commercial significance — as Rep. Barbour had predicted. Still, it managed to stay in business until 1918, and it paved the way for the privately funded Lee Highway two years later, which itself was incorporated into the first federal highway system as U.S. 11 six years after that.

The Wilderness Road broke off from the Great Valley Road and headed north into Kentucky at the Cumberland Gap, following a trail blazed by none other than Daniel Boone, who had been hired by the Transylvania Company to establish a foothold in the Native American lands west of Virginia.

You read that right: the Transylvania Company, a business formed by North Carolina judge Richard Henderson for the purpose of settling the region.

More than two centuries before Bram Stoker linked his famed vampire with the region of the same name in central Romania, the Transylvania Company played a key role in the expansion of the American colonies. In fact, for a brief time, it lay claim to an area in what would later become Kentucky and a portion of Tennessee that it touted as the 14th colony.

The name "Transylvania" is found elsewhere in the region, too: It's the name of a county in southwestern North Carolina, which was founded in 1861. The name, minus its vampiric overtones, simply refers to the land "beyond" or "across" (trans) "the forest" (sylvan).

Just two years later, in 1863, Judge Henderson employed Boone to scout out the land to the west. Boone made forays into the wilderness over the next few years, including one in 1773 in which he was attacked by indigenous people who killed his son, James. But things didn't begin to pick up until mid-March of 1775, when Henderson reached an agreement with the Overhill Cherokees, who obtained a wealth of goods in exchange for a vast swath of land that covered roughly half of modern Kentucky and a portion of Tennessee.

When it became clear the talks were about to bear fruit, Henderson dispatched Boone at the head of a 30-man team to blaze a trail through and beyond the Cumberland Gap, a mountain pass near the modern conjunction of Virginia, Tennessee, and Kentucky.

It was just that: a trail or bridle path, not broad or flat enough for wagons to navigate. Known first as Boone's Trace and later as the Wilderness Road, it was carved out through thickets and stands of tall trees, across rugged terrain and rivers like the Cumberland, Laurel, and Rockcastle — where the party had to swim to the other side when the waters rose. On April 1, 1775, Boone reached an open plain just over 15 miles southeast of modern

Lexington, where he set up a fort called Boone's Station (which later became known as Booneseboro). Henderson followed about a week later with a party of 40 mounted riflemen, together with slaves, supplies, cattle, and seed. Shortly after his arrival, he convened a constitutional convention for the proposed colony under the shade of a spreading elm, setting up three branches of government: legislative, executive, and judicial.

But there were complications. For one thing, the Overhill Cherokees weren't the only sovereign nation in the area, and others didn't recognize Henderson's claims. The Overhill contingent had warned Henderson that this would be a problem, and Boone himself was attacked while carving out the Wilderness Road before he even reached the site of Boone's Station.

A sketch by an anonymous artist shows the organizing convention for Transylvania Colony in May of 1775 in Boonesboro. *Public Domain*

That wasn't the end of the problems, either. The fort itself came under siege in 1776, 1777, and the late summer of 1778, when it was assailed by the forces of the British-allied Shawnee Nation. Boone himself was captured beforehand, but escaped, and his brother, Squire Boone, built a wooden cannon to help defend the fort. The Shawnees tried to burn it down, but rainy weather helped douse the flames, and they finally broke off the siege, retreating.

Boone left the settlement the following year, by which time the fort was secure but Henderson's dreams of establishing new colony had been dashed.

From the beginning, he'd had more than just the indigenous peoples to worry about.

Virginia insisted that much of the land he had purchased lay within its jurisdiction, and North Carolina laid a claim of its own. The Continental Congress refused to recognize the treaty Henderson had negotiated unless those colonies agreed to do so — something they weren't inclined to do.

In June of 1776, the Virginia General Assembly voted to deny the Transylvania Company any authority over settlers in the region, and within days, the 13 colonies had signed the Declaration of Independence, breaking away from England.

This was problematic because Henderson had relied on a British court decision that allowed a company to obtain title to land through treaty or negotiation (even as the crown retained sovereignty). The ruling applied to lands in India, but Henderson and others applied it to the American colonies, as well. Now, however, the colonies had declared independence, meaning they were no longer strictly bound by British legal precedents.

So it's no surprise that, in 1778, the Virginia Assembly declared Henderson's treaty null and void, granting him 200,000 acres of land along the Ohio River as compensation — an area that would become Henderson County, Kentucky.

Although the dream of Transylvania Colony was dead, the drive to settle the land itself was not. In addition to Boone's Station, others areas were settled around the same time. James Harrod ventured into the wilderness area by a different route, from Pennsylvania, and set up Harrod's Town (later Harrodsburg) in the summer of 1774; four years later, more than 50 people were living there, including Squire Boone. In 1776, Virginia militiaman Benjamin Logan set up a fort near the modern city of Stanford.

After the founding of Boone's Station, there were just over 100 people of European descent in the region; by 1790, that figure had grown to 75,000, and Kentucky was admitted to the Union two years later. Many of the settlers came in through the Wilderness Road. From 1775 to 1810, up to 300,000 people used the route to settle what would become the 15th state (Vermont beat it as No. 14 by a single year.)

Although it declined in importance later in the 19th century, the Wilderness Road was among the first in the United States to be paved — at least a section of it, from Cumberland Gap to Middlesboro, Kentucky. It which was modernized in 1908, at a time when less than 700 miles of U.S. roads were paved. It was later incorporated into the federal highway system as U.S. 25E.

The Wilderness Road was more than 200 miles long, starting in Virginia and winding its way up into Kentucky.

Above: Kane's Gap along the Wilderness Road, from *The Wilderness Road to Kentucky, Its Location and Features*, seen in 1921. *Public domain*

Left: Wilderness Road to Kentucky Pinnacle from Cumberland Gap, from *The Wilderness Road to Kentucky, Its Location and Features*, seen in 1919. *Public domain*

The entrance to the Cumberland Gap tunnel, top, and the view passing through, as seen in March 2021. *Author photos*.

Highway 25E, like the original Wilderness Road, wound its way up the mountain and through the saddleback pass known as Cumberland Gap. But all that changed in 1991, when workers began blasting their way through the mountain to carve out a pair of 30-foot-high tunnels that bypassed the mountain road. The $280 million project created two lanes of traffic going both ways for 4,600 feet — nearly nine-tenths of a mile.

When the tunnels opened more than five years after work began, local U.S. Rep. Hal Rogers called them "the most important thing that has happened here since Daniel Boone began to bring settlers through the Gap."

Cumberland Gap looking down on the town of Cumberland Gap, Tenn., from above, and up at the Gap from below. (The buildings are at bottom center of top photo). *Author photos.*

A plaque marks the path of the Wilderness Trail. It reads: "Indian Rock, Daniel Boone trail from North Carolina to Kentucky, 1775. Marked by St. Asaphs Chapter of Kentucky Daughters of the American Revolution, 1915." *Author photo.*

Once the tunnels were installed, the old paved highway road through the Gap was removed, and the mountain was restored to its natural state. The original Wilderness Trail was restored through the 20,000-acre national park that was authorized by Congress in 1940.

You can follow in Boone's footsteps over the trail, and you can still hike up the mountain (it's a little more than a mile) to see the Gap and gaze down on the small Tennessee town below. You can see where the road ends at the base of the mountain, where once it continued onward, winding as it rose upward and through the Gap to the other side.

But you won't be able to find the road. The restoration job was so complete that, even though it's been less than two decades since the road's been removed, as of this writing, one local said old-timers couldn't manage to locate where it once had been.

Other Paths

While Daniel Boone blazed a trail into what would later be called Kentucky, other roads made their way southward.

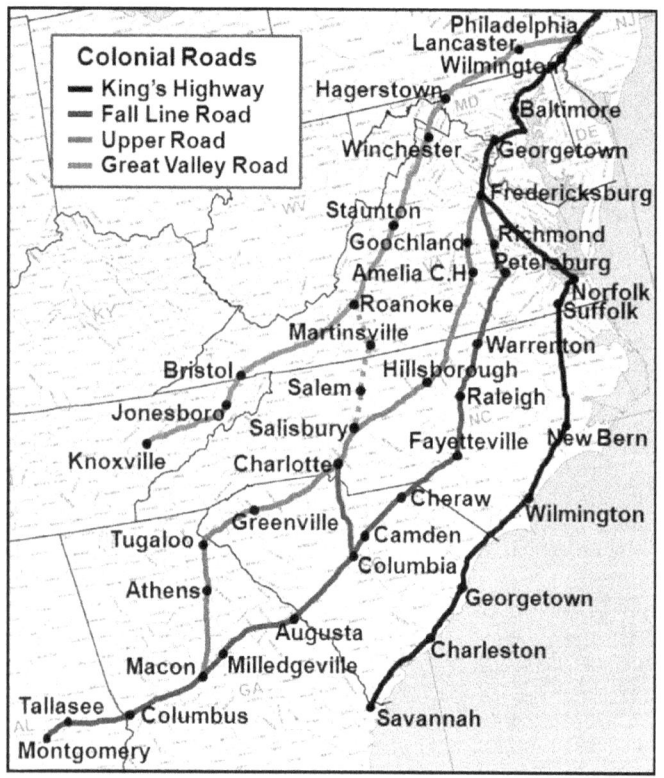

Colonial roads in the Southern United States. *Family History Research Wiki, public domain*

The Upper Road or Piedmont Road, and the Fall Line Road both branched off from the King's Highway at Fredericksburg, Virginia, and came back together in Macon, Georgia.

The Fall Line Road connected the growing mill towns of the interior. It followed the geographic dividing line between the Piedmont uplands and the coastal Tidewater plain because the rivers just above waterfalls along that route were easier to ford than mountain waterways or lowland marshes. The first roadway to link the inland settlements of Virginia and the Carolinas, the Fall Line Road passed through cities such as Richmond, Raleigh, Columbia, and Augusta.

The 580-mile Upper Road ran even farther inland. There's no modern equivalent to this old highway, now submerged beneath reservoirs in several places. It passed through such cities as Charlotte, Greenville, and Athens.

These roads were often called "stage" roads, for the stagecoaches that used them. Wagons changed their horses in stages along the way, usually at taverns — also called mile houses, because they were often built at one-mile intervals along the route. In addition to wagons, the roads were used to drive cattle and pigs from one place to another.

Several of these taverns still exist today, and you can still find a few mile markers, or milestones, from the early roads. If you travel down U.S. 31E in Kentucky, for example you can spot a couple of mile markers from its predecessor, the Louisville and Nashville Turnpike, a toll road built starting in 1837.

The road was heavily traveled in the mid-19th century before traffic declined with construction of the Louisville and Nashville Railroad, just before the Civil War. But portions of the pike later were used for the Dixie Highway, U.S. 31E and U.S. 31W.

HIGHWAYS OF THE SOUTH

The Old Stone Tavern in Atkins, Va., was built around 1815.
Author photo

Top and above: The Sherwood Inn, built starting in 1880, and a milestone outside on the old Louisville and Nashville Pike, U.S. 31E, New Haven, Ky.

Two views of the Talbott Tavern, which was built in 1779 in Bardstown, Ky. It has remained open continuously since then and is considered to be the oldest western stagecoach stop still operating. It sits near the town square on U.S. 31E. *Author photos*

Above: The Tavern in Abingdon, Va., sits on U.S. 11 and was founded in 1779.

Left: Mile stone north of Bardstown on U.S. 31E, the former route of the Louisville to Nashville Pike. *Author photos*

An old, bypassed section of the Louisville to Nashville Road south of Bardstown. *Author photo*

Farther to the south, a road built in the early 19th century largely followed an earlier Cherokee trading path across Cherokee lands in Georgia. The Georgia Road ran from Savannah northwest to Knoxville, Tennessee, and was one of two so-called Federal Roads in the South. The other passed through Creek lands, from a fort near Milledgeville, Georgia (then the state capital), to another near Mobile, Alabama. The Postal Department was in charge of the 1805 project, referred to as a "horse path" that followed an old Creek trading route.

HIGHWAYS OF THE SOUTH

Left: Sign marking the Old Federal Road (Georgia Road) in Rossville, Ga. *Author photo*

Below: U.S. government map from 1815, enhanced for readability, shows the path of federal roads. *Public domain*

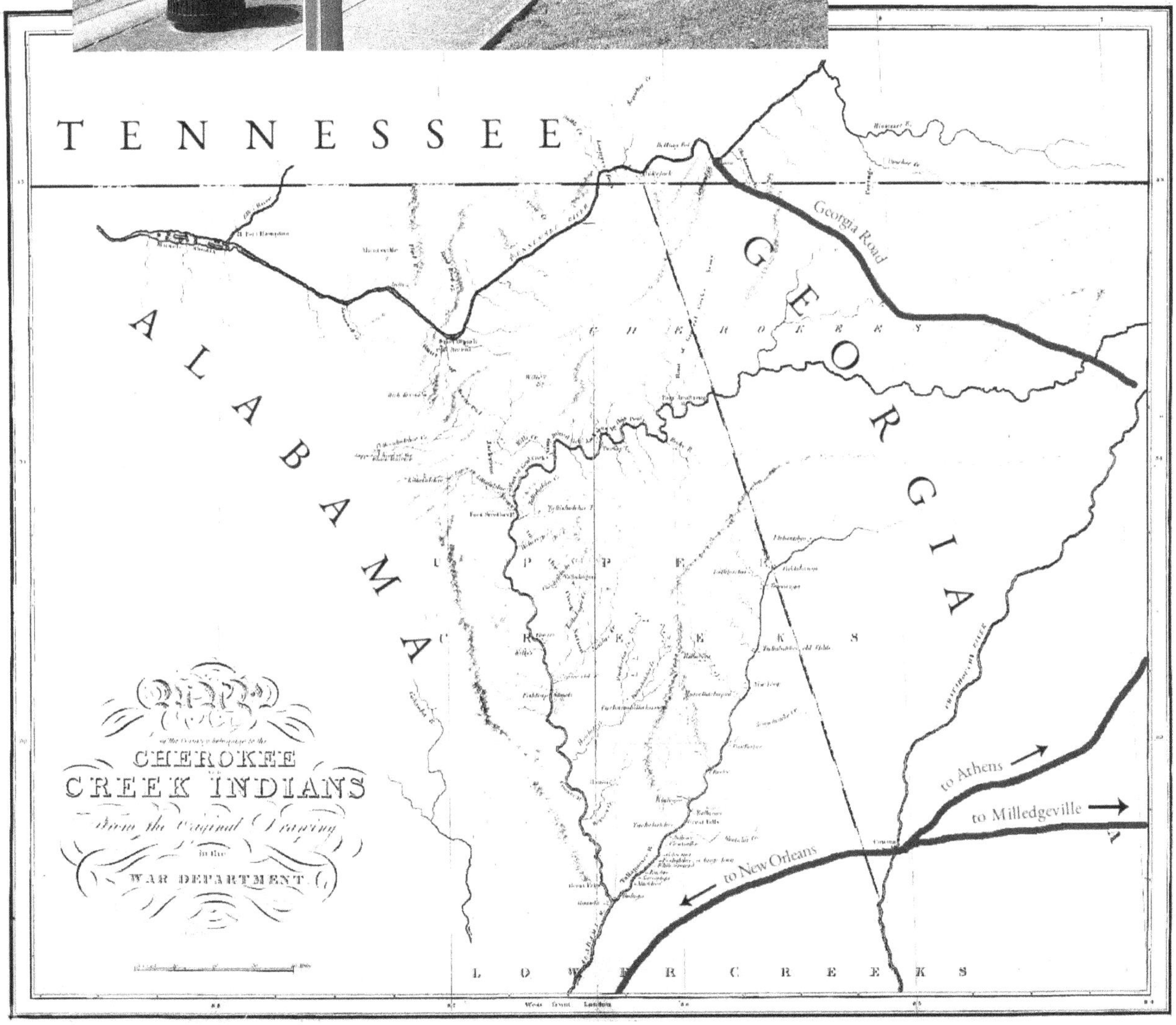

Selected Southern Trails

Name	Starting point	Destination	Open
King's Highway	Boston	Charleston, S.C.	1650
Fall Line Road	Fredericksburg, Va.	Macon, Ga.	1735
Natchez Trace	Natchez, Miss.	Nashville, Tenn.	1742
Great Valley Road	Philadelphia	Augusta, Ga.	1744
Upper Road	Fredericksburg, Va.	Macon, Ga.	1748
Wilderness Road	Cumberland Gap	Lexington, Ky.	1775
Zane's Trace	Wheeling, W.Va.	Maysville, Ky.	1805
Federal Road (Georgia)	Savannah, Ga.	Knoxville, Tenn.	1805
Federal Road (Alabama)	Milledgeville, Ga.	Mobile, Ala.	1805

Speaking of horse paths, many roads in the South remained little more than that well into the 20th century. Just 2,100 out of 48,000 miles of road in North Carolina (slightly over 4 percent) were paved with gravel or macadam in 1912; the rest was dirt — or mud, depending on the season.

Railroads, though in decline, still provided the most reliable way of getting from one place to another at any distance: More than 1,500 cities and towns in the state had rail stations, making it a simple matter to travel in comfort from one place to another, then catch a streetcar to wherever it was you'd booked a room.

The Good Roads movement had been founded in the 19th century to tout the benefits of well-paved roads to travelers and, crucially, farmers seeking to get their crops to market, but progress had been slow. The federal and state governments had stayed largely on the sidelines, leaving road-building to the counties and private interests. The counties often didn't coordinate with one another, leaving roads to dead-end at the county line. And the private interests had their own agenda.

Highway associations began to form in the early 1910s, run by businessmen keen on directing traffic to their establishments. The resulting highways — referred to as "auto trails"— tended to be zigzag affairs, eschewing direct routes in favor of paths that served the interests of their sponsors. Lengthy sections were left unpaved, so travelers had to take their chances and hope for the best. Louisiana, for example, was home to a hodgepodge of disconnected trails and "earth roads" used mostly for horse-drawn wagons and livestock.

Dirt roads in Georgia show how difficult it could be to get from one place to another during and shortly after rains. *Library of Congress*

Over the next few years, major auto trails were planned and at least partially built through the South, with names honoring the likes of Thomas Jefferson, Andrew Jackson, Alabama Senator John Bankhead, and Confederate figures Jefferson Davis, and Robert E. Lee. There was also a Dixie Highway (actually a network of roads) running from Michigan to Miami, which was not to be confused with the Dixie Overland Highway, an east-west road from Savannah, Georgia, to San Diego.

The Bankhead, Lee, and Jefferson Davis highways all started in or near Washington, D.C., and followed different paths westward to San Diego. The Jackson and Jefferson highways were north-south roads to New Orleans, with their northern endpoints in Chicago and Winnipeg, Canada, respectively.

The most celebrated auto trail, the Lincoln Highway, didn't run through the South, but rather, across the Midwest, linking New York and San Francisco. It had the financial backing of Goodyear Tire and the Packard motor car company behind it, but it still fell far short of paving its entire 3,000-plus-mile length. Indeed, it adopted a strategy of paving "seedling miles" to demonstrate what the end product would look like... once it got enough donations to pay for it all. (By 1938, a dozen years after the highway had been superseded by various federal highways, 42 miles still remained to be paved in something better than gravel.)

Other auto trails faced similar funding challenges, and other rural roads remained largely unpaved, as well. By 1921, there were 136,000 cars registered in North Carolina, but that was still less than 1.5 percent of the national total. In wintertime, roads were washed out as a matter of routine during rainstorms, and travelers who did have cars risked getting stuck in the mud. The situation was similar across the South, and throughout the country in general.

In 1916, just five states (none of them in the South) possessed even one trans-state highway. That same year, the federal government passed legislation promising matching funds to states that improved their road systems, but those funds were capped at $10,000 a mile. That might sound like a lot — until you consider that it cost that much just to pave a mile just in gravel, and four times as much ($40,000 a mile) to pave it in concrete. Then, the United States' entry into World War I that same overshadowed domestic priorities for the next two years.

After the war ended, states started to look for ways to access those federal matching funds — especially after the federal government passed a more expansive highways act in 1921. It wasn't long before they hit on a dependable method: gasoline taxes. Oregon was the first to pass one, in 1919, and it wasn't long before other states adopted the same approach. Kentucky became the first Southern state to pass a fuel tax a year later, and Georgia, North Carolina, Louisiana, Florida, and Arkansas followed suit in 1921.

Still, that year, only 25 states were building permanent, mostly gravel, roads.

HIGHWAYS OF THE SOUTH

The Lee Highway followed the path of the old Great Valley Road in Virginia. Some portions remained unpaved in 1920, when these photos were taken by the Lee Highway Association in Virginia. *Library of Congress*

More photos taken by the Lee Highway Association in Virginia, 1920, show a smooth road, but one of compressed earth and gravel, not concrete. *Library of Congress*

HIGHWAYS OF THE SOUTH

Bad roads were so common that the pioneering Piggly Wiggly grocery chain used them as a metaphor for the evils of credit that appeared in a 1923 newspaper ad published across the South. The ad told the story of a driver whose wagon "became stuck fast in a muddy road."

"If the wagon of your finances is stuck in the bog of credit," the ad proclaimed, you had no one to blame but yourself. But if you paid cash, you'd "stay off the muddy road."

The Piggly Wiggly road was "smooth and surfaced and straight. There are not bogs of credit, not ruts, and no holes of needless expense. Travel on it always, and you'll arrive ahead of time."

In 1925, only 225 miles of out of 4,740 in South Carolina were paved, even though it has passed a gas tax of 2 cents a gallon three years earlier — double what most other states had adopted.

It wasn't enough, as the lack of progress made clear. By 1925, it had raised the level to 5 cents a gallon, the highest in the nation.

A car is stuck in high water along the South Carolina coast in 1924. *Library of Congress*

By that same year, North Carolina had used a mixture of gasoline taxes, highway bonds, and licensing fees to build 7,680 miles of hard-topped roads. The state had passed a $50 million road-construction bond in 1921, the same year it approved a penny-a-gallon gas tax, on March 3. It had raised that to 4 cents a gallon by 1925, the same level seen in Arkansas and Florida. Indeed, by then, every state in the South had some kind of fuel tax.

Oil companies, predictably, challenged the taxes in court, contending that they were unconstitutional property taxes. The courts, however, ruled that they were excise taxes on a specific product. The Arkansas Supreme Court turned aside a challenge by Standard Oil, stating: "The thing which is really taxed is the use of the vehicle... upon the public highway... The extent of the use," the ruling continued, "is measured by the quantity of fuel consumed, and the tax is imposed according to the extent of the use thus measured."

The federal highway system was established the following year.

North Carolina's roads were abysmal before the passage of the state's first gas tax in 1921. From top in 1920: "An argument for adequate maintenance law" in Haywood County; a deep cut in Polk County; and the main highway between Spruce Pine and Burnsville in Yancey County.
N.C. State Highway Commission

Working to improve North Carolina highways in 1920. **Top:** Topeka surfacing on a federal aid project in Buncombe County. **Above:** Bituminous surface spreading in Wake County. *N.C. State Highway Commission*

By 1922, roads in North Carolina were starting to look a lot better. Some were smoothly paved, with wooden guardrails and center lines, like these two stretches. **Top:** Chapel Hill Boulevard in Durham. **Above:** Durham County federal highway project. *N.C. State Highway Commission*

Bennett's Mill Bridge, build in 1855, carries East Tygart's Creek Road (County Road 1215) over Tygart's Creek in Lynn, Greenup County, Ky. *Library of Congress*

Bridging Gaps

Having roads was a good thing, until something got in the way. Then you needed a way to get over, under, or through it — rivers and streams being the most common obstacles.

The best way to get past them was to build a bridge.

Most of the nation's oldest bridges are in the Northeast, but you can find a few of them in the South.

South Carolina, is the site of the region's oldest bridge: an abandoned arch span that dates to 1782. John Seabrook built the bridge over a branch of the Wadmalaw River to connect his stagecoach tavern and ferry landing to the city of Charleston. It's one of just two brick bridges in Charleston County to have been built before the Civil War.

Looking across an old concrete bridge next to U.S. 11 near Abingdon, Va., date of construction unknown. Author photo

The Royals Springs Bridge in Kentucky's Scott County is a stone arch bridge that was built starting in 1800 over Royal Spring Creek. And the old River Road Bridge can be found in Jefferson County, also in Kentucky to the west. It's not clear when that one was built, but since a new bridge went up right next to it in 1935, it must date to at least the first part of the 20th century.

The Goose Creek Bridge is yet another stone arch bridge — the most common type in those days. This bridge near U.S. 50 in Loudon County, Virginia, dates to 1802, and carried traffic all the way up to 1957. The Elk Grove Stone Bridge, on the other hand, still supports a modern road (U.S. 40) in Wheeling, West Virginia. It was built over Little Wheeling Creek all the way back in 1817, and was widened in 1931, when sidewalks and railings were also added.

Two more stone arch bridges in the South date to 1820: The Hibbs Bridge in Loudon County, Virginia, and the Poinsett Bridge in Greenville County, South Carolina.

As time passed, though, builders started constructing covered bridges from wood. Wooden bridges were easier to build, but they were also less durable, especially when exposed to harsh weather. The timber-truss roof shielded a bridge from the elements, which helped preserve it, although the roof itself had to be replaced every 10 to 20 years.

HIGHWAYS OF THE SOUTH

The nation's first covered bridge went up in Philadelphia in 1805, and the design proved so popular that 14,000 of them have been built since. Most of them went up in the Northeast and Midwest, where weather could be the harshest, but a good number were built in the South, as well, mostly during the from 1820 to 1870. At that point, more builders began constructing steel truss and concrete arch bridges: They were stronger and lasted longer. By 2005, just 900 covered bridges remained, most of them in Ohio and Pennsylvania.

Others have disappeared since. The 80-foot-long Bob White Covered Bridge in rural Virginia had stood since 1921 when it was washed away in 2015 by a flood following six consecutive days of rainfall. It was one of just half a dozen covered bridges left in the state, and one of two in the small town of Woolwine, off State Route 8.

Sixteen covered bridges were left in Georgia as of 2020, all built in 1915 or earlier; the Red Oak Creek Bridge, built by a slave named Horace King, dates back to 1840. King, an architect and engineer, also built bridges in Alabama (where he helped design the state capitol) and Mississippi. A dozen covered spans remained in Kentucky, including Bennett's Mill Bridge, built in 1855. There were 11 in Alabama, and 10 in Mississippi, while Tennessee had half a dozen, North Carolina two, and South Carolina just one.

Covered bridge spanning the Maury River in Lexington, Va. *Library of Congress*

Top: Covered bridge near Eatonton, Ga., in 1936. *Library of Congress*

Right: Buzzard Roost Covered Bridge, Colbert County, Ala. *Library of Congress*

Left: A man walks out of a covered bridge in Trent's Mills, Va., in 1933. *Library of Congress*

Top: Bridge over the South Fork of the Licking River in Cynthiana, Ky., 1934. *Library of Congress*

Above: Jack's Creek Bridge in Woolwine, Va., was built in 1914. The 48-foot span is just off State Route 8. *Author photo*

Top: Watsonville Bridge in Madison County, Ga., spans the South Fork of the Broad River. The state's longest covered bridge, it was built in 1885 by Washington W. King, son of slave and bridge architect Horace King. *Library of Congress*

Above and right: Bunker Hill Covered Bridge, one of two covered bridges left in North Carolina. *Author photos*

HIGHWAYS OF THE SOUTH

Right: This concrete arch bridge on Wentworth Street near Reidsville, N.C., dates to 1922.

Below: Concrete arch bridge over the Dan River in Danville, Va. *Author photos*

Above: The John Snodgrass Bridge, a cantilevered truss span over the Tennessee River on State Route 117 in Alabama, was completed in 1958.

Right: Old Elkton Bridge in Tennessee, at left in photo, was built in 1924 and replaced by a parallel span in 1959. Below are good-luck horseshoes in concrete at the site. *Author photos*

City Centers

U.S. Business Route 220 through Madison, N.C., 2021. *Author photo*

Down on Main Street

The history of highways begins with the railroads, which formed the nation's first extensive road system. It even has the word "road" in its name: The cars just run on rails instead of asphalt or concrete. The railroads were what first connected the major cities of North America, and that only made sense: Before the motorcar was invented, you couldn't get from New York to San Francisco or Chicago or Atlanta by walking or with a horse and buggy.

A wagon train might do the trick, if you were a pioneer or homesteader setting out over open fields into uncharted territory, but the railroad was the first system dedicated to transporting passengers and freight between America's largest cities. What roads existed — with the exception of a few privately funded toll roads such as the Valley Pike through Virginia's Shenandoah Valley — were strictly local. They were spokes on a wheel, the hub of which was the train station in town.

Indeed, new towns that weren't seaports or riverports in the mid-19th century sprang up largely along rail lines. The depot became the focal point of downtown, which sprang up around it. Industrial plants and mills, whether they processed cotton, tobacco, lumber, or steel, arrayed themselves around train stations so they could load and unload their products quickly and easily. Retailers selling those products and set up shop nearby, as did restaurants, barbers, liquor stores, post offices, and hotels.

Above: Tracks in the commercial section of Dillon, S.C., beside the Dillon County Theatre and Chamber of Commerce (colonnade). *Author photo*

Right: San Angelo, Texas, Santa Fe depot, 1865. *Library of Congress*

Depots in Bassett (top) and Rocky Mount, Va., both sit close to the town center, even today. The Bassett depot is alongside State Route 57, while the Rocky Mount station is near the intersection of State Route 40 and old U.S. 220. *Author photos*

What roads there were just gave farmers a way to get to and from the cities, where they could unload their raw agricultural products and pick up what they needed for their home life. This interplay, between the depot as hub and farms as the endpoints of each spoke, formed the basis of the American economy in the second half of the 19th century. As John Moody, founder of Moody's Investment Services, put it, the United States was "largely the result of mechanical inventions, and in particular of agricultural machinery and the railroad. One transformed millions of acres of uncultivated land into fertile farms, while the other furnished the transportation which carried the crops to distant markets."

String bean pickers wait for trucks to pick them up by an RC Cola sign along the highway near Gibson, La., in October 1938. *Lee Russell, Library of Congress*

Nowhere was this truer, or for longer, than in the South. Its agrarian economy was dependent on slavery and, later, sharecropping — a system under which tenants gave a share of the crop they grew to farm owners, in exchange for the right to live on the land. It was a meager existence, and many sharecroppers (poor white farmers and newly freed slaves) were forced to sign oppressive contracts that left them dirt poor just so they could have a place to stay.

These systems preserved the rural character of the South, and ensured that Southern life centered on the farm, not the city.

HIGHWAYS OF THE SOUTH

Scenes from Southern highways illustrate the rural character of life in the region in these photos taken by Marion Post Wolcott in 1939. **Top:** A woman carrying laundry along highway between Durham and Mebane, N.C. **Above:** Cotton fallen from wagons (foreground) lies beside U.S. Highway 49 in Mississippi. *Library of Congress photos*

Largest cities in the South, 1920

In 1920, only a handful of Southern cities, including four in Texas, boasted a population of 100,000 or more.

Rank	City	State	Population
17	New Orleans	Louisiana	387,219
33	Atlanta	Georgia	200,616
36	Birmingham	Alabama	178,806
38	Richmond	Virginia	171,667
40	Memphis	Tennessee	162,351
41	San Antonio	Texas	161,379
42	Dallas	Texas	158,976
45	Houston	Texas	138,276
56	Nashville	Tennessee	118,342
59	Norfolk	Virginia	115,777
65	Fort Worth	Texas	106,482

Cities themselves were small: so much so that, as the automobile was coming of age in 1920, the only city in the Deep South that ranked among the nation's 20 largest was the port city of New Orleans, at No. 17. St. Louis, Kansas City, and Louisville all were in the top 30, but they were on the fringes of the region, as much Midwestern as Southern in character. Washington, D.C., which ranked 14th and isn't included on this list, was, similarly, a blend of Southern style and mid-Atlantic metropolitanism.

The rural character of the South kept people isolated from one another, except when they attended church or delivered their crops to market. Beyond that, most of them had neither the time nor any use for city life. Black sharecroppers weren't welcome in the city; if they were white, they couldn't afford to spend any time or money there.

Transportation was a problem, too: More than 30 percent of U.S. farmers had automobiles in 1920, including nearly half of those in the North. In the South, though, it was a different story: Fewer than 15 percent of them did. Trucks, and even tractors, were less common in the South than elsewhere, despite a heavy reliance on agriculture, and although the numbers would increase with time, the region still lagged behind the North and West in all three categories 30 years later.

Cotton was king in the Deep South, and would reach its peak in terms of acreage at end of the 1920s. Southern Louisiana was largely dedicated to sugar beets, with rice being grown there, too, as well as in South Carolina. Soybeans and sweet potatoes could be found across the South, while peanuts were concentrated in Georgia, Mississippi, and the Tidewater region along the Virginia-North Carolina state line. Apples were grown in Appalachia, while tobacco was the top crop in the Carolinas and Virginia.

But the cities, though smaller than their northern counterparts, were increasingly ruled by the automobile. There were 20,000 cars each in Atlanta, Memphis, and New Orleans, with 16,000 in Birmingham and 12,000 in Nashville. They were a boon to city businesses, but it wasn't always heralded as progress by those who saw them as a threat to their way of life.

Older homes in neighborhoods near city centers were often torn down to make way for wider streets and new businesses that catered to motorists, like filling stations and garages. (Ironically, many of these were abandoned decades later or transformed into other roadside businesses, ranging from dry cleaners to coffeehouses.)

An old gas station in downtown Reidsville, N.C., had found new life as a hot dog stand by 2020. *Author photo*

An old Pure Oil station on U.S. 11 in Lexington, Va., was operating in 2020 as Pure Eats, with a menu featuring doughnuts, burgers, shakes, and craft beer. *Author photo*

Then there was the traffic. City streets had been designed for local traffic, specifically, horse carriages. But as highways replaced railroads as the primary means of connecting cities with one another, "Main Streets" became the lynchpins that held them together — and the bottlenecks where town folk and visitors vied for finite segments of roadway.

One speaker described the situation in a 1929 address to the Presidents' Club of Atlanta as follows: "From the moment your car hits the edge of Peachtree (Street), it is touch and go, jostle and jump, 'horn in' fast and then throw your wife abruptly through the windshield by suddenly braking down."

Other Southern cities faced similar problems.

Among the ideas for dealing with the congestion was a new invention called the automatic signal. In the fall of 1924, the *Chattanooga Daily Times* reported that leading experts were hailing it as the most successful system for eliminating traffic jams. By that time, it had already been installed in cities such as Dallas (where it was first introduced),

Houston, Shreveport, Louisville, New Orleans, and Birmingham.

"The colors are red for stop, green for go, and amber for clearing of intersections. A bell rings each time the signal changes, or while the amber light is burning. All pedestrians are required to clear out of the intersection during the amber light, which remains on for thirty seconds."

The situation was far different then, before interstates were built. Modern freeways bypass towns along the way, and travelers use "business" or "alternate" routes to access them. But those routes are, in most cases, the original highways: the ones that went through towns rather than around them.

> **SOMETIMES IT'S GREEN, SOMETIMES IT'S RED.**
> **IF YOU START ACROSS, YOU MIGHT BE DEAD.**
> Henry Vance, Birmingham News columnist, 1924

The traffic signals described in the *Chattanooga Daily Times* must have seemed like a modern marvel in 1924, but they only solved the problem temporarily, as highways funneled more and more cars into cities. Two years later, the first federal highway system created formal links between city streets and rural highways, directing traffic along dedicated routes marked by black-and-white shields.

In Roanoke, Virginia, for example, U.S. 460 traced a section of Melrose Avenue, while U.S. 11 followed Campbell Avenue for a short distance downtown. In Asheville, North Carolina, Merrimon and Biltmore avenues became U.S. 25. Government Street through Mobile, Alabama, served as the basis for the Jefferson Davis Highway, which later became U.S. 90, and U.S. 51 in Jackson, Mississippi, followed State Street north out of town toward Memphis.

Entering Dallas, 1942. *Arthur Rothstein, Library of Congress*

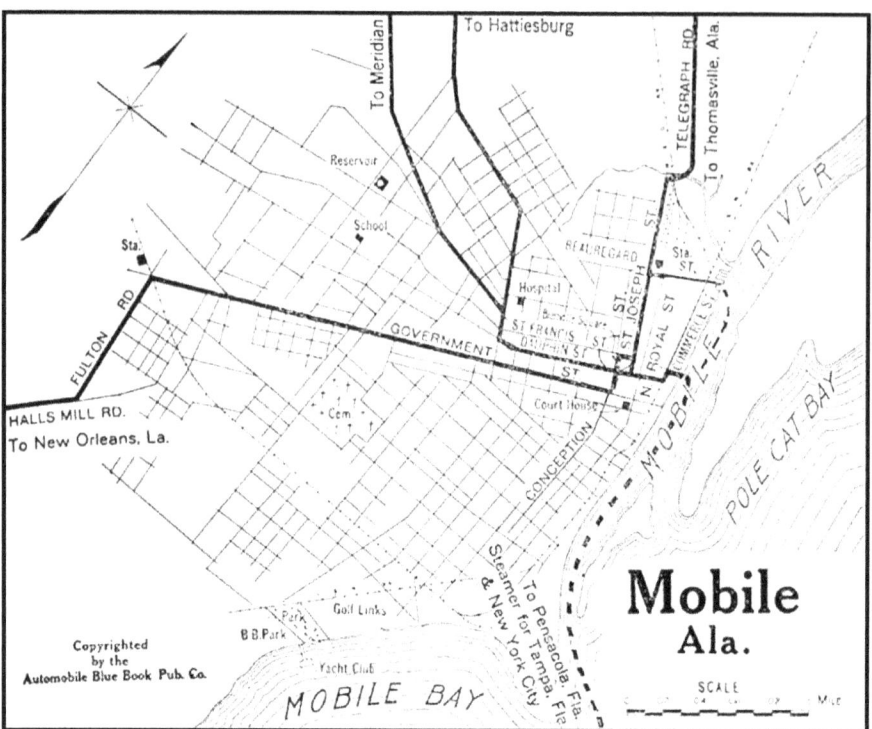

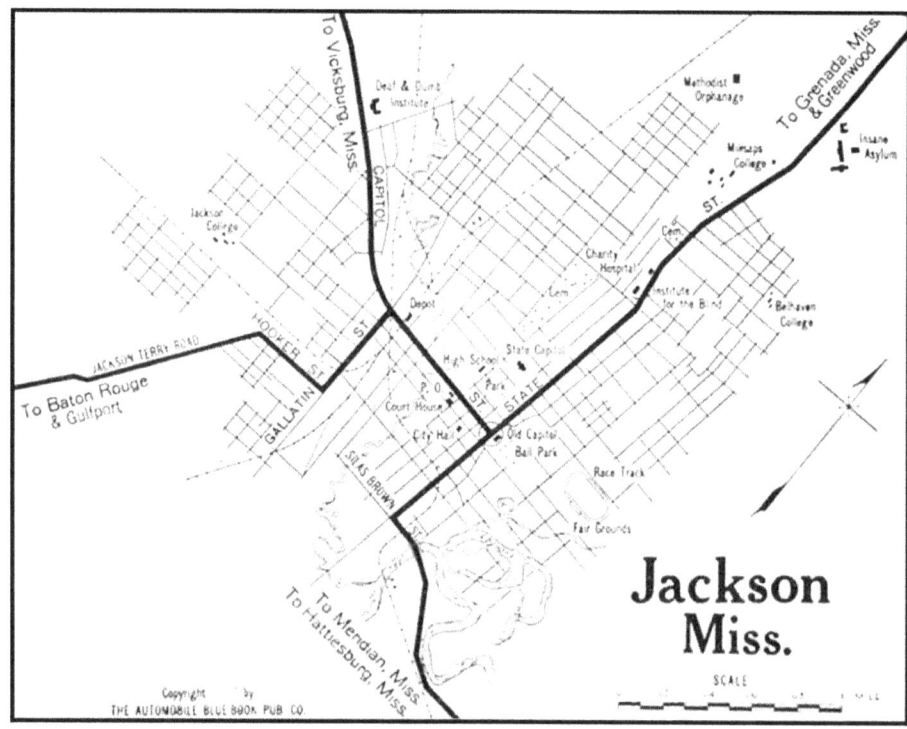

Maps from the 1919 Automobile Blue Book show Government Street, future U.S. 90, in Mobile, Ala., and State Street, future U.S. 51, in Jackson, Miss. *Public domain*

HIGHWAYS OF THE SOUTH

Intersections could get busy in the city, especially if you had to stop and figure out which way you were headed.

Above: Innovations like the traffic signal helped, but by the time this photo was taken in Little Rock, Ark., in 1958, the new interstate highway system was badly needed. *Thomas J. O'Halloran, Library of Congress*

Left: A marker at the center of an intersection in Crossville, Tenn., points to multiple destinations in 1937. *Arthur Rothstein, Library of Congress*

As highways linked up in downtowns, more people were using them in more cars than ever before. By the end of the 1920s, vehicle registrations had more than tripled in Atlanta, Memphis, and New Orleans in the span of a decade. They'd grown nearly that fast in Memphis, and they'd more than quadrupled in Birmingham. The signals that had been installed to manage traffic were instead creating logjams, which was fine for businesses along the way, which had a captive audience, but was no fun for travelers and commuters caught in the bottleneck.

In cities with electric trolleys — and there were many in the South — the problem was even worse.

"Traffic congestion is unspeakable," said J.N. Shannahan of the American Electric Railway Association. "It is virtually impossible nowadays, be reason of traffic congestion, to maintain any respectable schedule on our city streets… Oftentimes, one person in a single vehicle will get out in front of a (trolley) car and delay 60 persons in it merely by occupying the track."

It turned out to be a losing battle, as many electric streetcar companies went out of business in the 1930s, though some stuck it out through the 1940s or even the '50s.

Traffic in Horse Cave, Ky., July 1940. *Marion Post Wolcott, Library of Congress*

A statue of Abraham Lincoln sits at the center of the town square on U.S. 31E in Hodgenville, Ky., near the president's birthplace. *Author photo*

At that point, city streets were so congested, no one was happy. Cities had been built on one of two templates: Some had been created beside rail lines, with the depot serving as the central focus. Others were developed around a town square, usually with a courthouse in the middle, surrounded by key retailers like a barbershop, pharmacy, grocery store, and stables.

But neither of those models worked in the automotive age. The railway station had been at the center of some towns for good reason in the early days: It was where goods were delivered and shipped out, and it was the only way for people to travel long distances. As the 20th century progressed, however, highways replaced rail cars as a means of personal travel, while big rigs accounted for more and more long-distance freight transport.

The town square, meanwhile, became an outdated relic. Some cities outgrew the old courthouses and built new ones away from the city center. Retailers moved out to the suburbs. And motorists, who no longer had anywhere to go downtown, did whatever they could to avoid slowing down at the square to get from one side of town to the other.

Americans needed a workaround, so they skirted the towns altogether with the new interstate highway system and other bypasses added to the federal and various state systems.

Downtowns declined even further, the suburbs prospered, and drivers zipped merrily along, oblivious to it all.

The Hotel Patten in Chattanooga was at the center of it all. U.S. highways 41, 11, and 27 all met out front at this five-way intersection. You can just imagine the congestion. The Dixie Highway Association held its first meeting at the hotel in 1915, because Chattanooga was at the midway point between the Great Lakes and Florida. Eventually, two legs of the highway converged there before branching off again. The building is seen here in 2021. *Author photo*

Above: Downtown Roanoke, Va., in 2020.

Right: The old Bardstown, Ky., courthouse in the town square at U.S. 31E, was built in 1892 and served as a visitor center by the time this photo was taken in 2021. *Author photos*

Right: Downtown in Mebane, a small North Carolina town lined with telephone poles, 2021.

Below: The city center in Knoxville, Tenn., 2019. *Author photos*

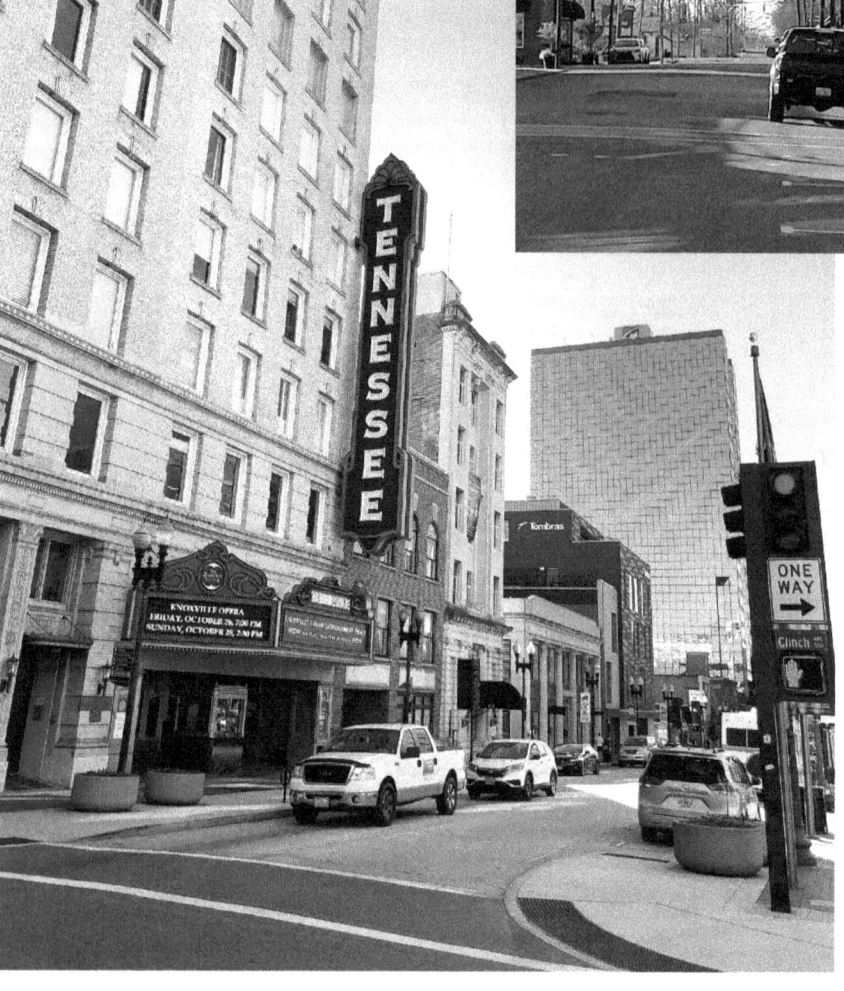

Above: Downtown in Mt. Airy, N.C., the town on which Mayberry in *The Andy Griffith Show* is based, 2019.

Right: Clocktower at the railroad tracks in Dillon, Ga., 2019. *Author photos*

An obelisk honoring Zebulon Baird Vance, governor of North Carolina during the Civil War and a U.S. senator from 1880 to 1894, rises at the city center in Asheville, N.C. Construction began in 1897. A Dixie Highway marker, inset, stands near the base. *Author photos*

Historic city halls in Jacksonville, Fla. (above) and Savannah, Ga., as seen in 2019. *Author photos*

City scenes from Dallas, top, in 1942 and Spartanburg, S.C., in 1943. *Library of Congress*

HIGHWAYS OF THE SOUTH

Top and left: Library of Congress photos show main streets in Alexandria, La., in 1940 and Norfolk, Va., 1941.

Above: Cumberland Gap, Tenn., 2021. *Author photo*

Top: Main Street in Crane, Texas, in May 1939. Lee Russell, Library of Congress
Above: Downtown Bristol, Va., in 2021. *Author photo*

Above: Old City Hall, Richmond, Va., in 2019.

Left: Woolworth Building, Atlanta, 2018. *Author photos*

The Stringers Ridge Tunnel on Cherokee Boulevard (State Route 8), was completed in 1908, giving motorists a direct shot into downtown Chattanooga. *Author photo*

Old-Time Religion

Religious sign along a Georgia highway in May 1939. *Marion Post Wolcott, Library of Congress*

Highway to Heaven

Faith has always played a major role in Southern life, so it's no wonder that's reflected along the highways and country roads that crisscross the region. From billboards to yard signs, from country churches to tent revivals, the highway to heaven often runs parallel to the earthly highways of the South.

The Bible Belt and the South itself are all but synonymous, with evangelical churches most prominent. In 2015, Tennessee led the way, with more one-third of adults belonging to the Baptist tradition, and more than half overall (52 percent) identifying as evangelicals. The numbers in Alabama were only slightly lower, and across the South, just more than a third of adults called themselves evangelicals. Overall, more than three-quarters of Southerners were Christians. No other region approached those figures.

Southern-Style Faith

Religion developed in the South in part as a reaction to the elitism of Anglicanism, which was the official religion in the colonial era. Ministers were unmoved by the day-to-day struggles of the commonfolk, from whom they remained distant — not just spiritually, but literally: The front pews were paid for by aristocrats, like box seats at a sporting event, with the lower classes, mostly small-scale planters, relegated to the cheap seats.

The ministers weren't paid by parishioners, but by the government via tobacco taxes, which insulated them further from the concerns of those in the pews. In light of this, it was natural for parishioners to run for the exits once America declared independence. The influence of the Anglican Church faded quickly, and three other denominations — Presbyterians, Methodists, and Baptists — filled the void. Without any official backing, they had to compete for converts, and in doing so recognized the importance of responding to the concerns of rural believers.

The kind of distant, structured ritual that catered to aristocrats held no appeal to them. They wanted a faith that was relevant to their lives, and were less interested in doctrine than in experiencing the divine. They had no use for a remote paint-by-numbers tradition built to reinforce a rigid class system and assuage the consciences of those with money and social standing. They wanted a personal, dynamic faith and fellowship.

The kind of faith that developed was geared toward a direct, familiar relationship with Jesus, whose given name was often preferred to the more formal title of "Christ" uttered in old-line congregations. Emphasis came to be was placed on inner communion with the Holy Spirit, rather than outer, doctrinal concerns.

Liturgies and calendar-based readings, assigned by date and season, were largely abandoned. Instead, preachers delivered sermons as they were "moved by the Spirit." The imminence of the divine came to be expressed in a sort of living liturgy: activities modeled after the acts and marvels recorded in the New Testament. This was especially true in Pentecostal churches. In addition to holy communion, various congregations would practice foot-washing, speak "in tongues," praying for (and expecting) miraculous healings, and even — in the case of some Appalachian churches beginning in the early 20th century — handling poisonous snakes in fulfillment of a verse in the Book of Mark. Baptism was done by immersion, rather than by sprinkling water on the believer's head.

Again, that's how it was done in the New Testament, specifically by John the Baptist, who baptized Jesus in the Jordan River.

As experience replaced doctrine as the defining element of Southern religious life, it created a bond that was far more powerful than the kind of connection formed through writ or ritual. Based on emotion rather than reason or tradition, it was a manifestation of the living God within, not mere obedience to a set of precepts handed down across generations.

This kind of living faith rendered doctrine itself secondary, and allowed a kind of flexibility not available in more traditional churches. Each individual could define his faith based on personal experience — and, significantly, cultural priorities. It was this sort of flexibility that allowed Southern believers to create a distinctive brand of Christianity that affirmed their cultural identity in a way the old Anglicans or distrusted Catholics never could. (Anti-Catholic sentiment was strong in the South, and was fomented by the KKK at the height of its powers in the early 1920s.)

In practical terms, this meant that Christianity could be used as an excuse to buttress cultural priorities ranging from slavery to temperance. Doctrine wasn't the point; salvation was. This attitude was expressed in the common refrain, "We have no creed but Christ, no book but the Bible, no name but Christian."

Denominations were less important than a simple confession of faith, and a multitude of church groups arose to replace the monolithic Church of England. The largest group, the Baptists, were a loose collection of locally governed congregations, rather than a top-down hierarchy. The largest group, the Southern Baptists, were joined by the likes of Free Will Baptists, Primitive Baptists, Missionary Baptists, and others. Pentecostals sorted themselves out into Assemblies of God, the Tennessee-based Church of God, the Foursquare Church, Pentecostal Holiness Church, Calvary Chapel, and others.

All these churches had one thing in common: They were evangelical. A cornerstone of their theology, as mentioned, was salvation. But they didn't wait for sinners to come to them, they followed Jesus' "great commission" from the Gospel of Matthew to "go and make disciples of all nations, baptizing them in the name of the Father and of the Son and of the Holy Spirit, and teaching them to obey everything I have commanded you."

Highways provided them with a way to do just that. Churches were built, but they were mostly small and modest, in contrast to the ornate and luxurious cathedrals of Europe.

Typical Southern roadside churches, from top: Mount Bethel United Methodist in Bahama, N.C.; Christian View Pentecostal Holiness Church off U.S. 220 at the North Carolina-Virginia state line; Christ's Church, Martinsville, Va. *Author photos*

HIGHWAYS OF THE SOUTH

Modest churches such as the wooden church at left, seen in 1936 on the sealevel highway south of Charleston, S.C, and a chapel in Ridgeway, Va., (below left), contrast with the more elaborate structure of the First Baptist Church in Knoxville, Tenn.

Library of Congress, top left; author photos above left and above.

Roadside Revivals

Even today, country churches in the South are mostly humble, with little to distinguish one from another, at least outwardly. Early buildings were often like cabins with little more than crude bell towers or crosses to identify them as places of worship. Brick and stone were common as well, and the sight of a red brick church with a modest colonnade on the front porch and a white steeple pointing the way toward heaven became a common sight along Southern byways.

The church, evangelicals preached, wasn't a building at all, but the people themselves. And the experience of fellowship could be had just as easily outdoors as in a building. That experience centered on salvation, and redemption, the act of committing one's life to Jesus. New believers were as likely to be baptized in local streams as indoors. And meetings often took place not in churches themselves, but in roadside tent revival meetings meant to attract the wayfaring (and wayward) sinner who happened to walk or drive past.

Traveling preachers took their show on the road, following in the footsteps of itinerants from the 18th and 19th centuries, but now setting up shop along the highways in search of souls to save. Few of them had formal seminary training; they were better known for their charisma and their fiery messages.

Some weren't exactly models of moral rectitude. In 1927, a roving preacher who went by an alias was arrested in Virginia charged with setting fire to 14 buildings to collect insurance money. His stepson turned him in. An itinerant in Birmingham was jailed for killing a Catholic priest, and a preacher in Tennessee named W.B. Hurst was convicted of bigamy for "having too many wives," the *Bristol Herald Courier* reported in 1922:

"About one year ago he married a lady in this county and lived with her until a short time ago, when it was learned that he was wanted in several other places on a charge of bigamy. He confessed to having one or more living wives and the proof showed he had been married nine times. Several of the women could not be located, and Hurst was reluctant to discuss them in court."

He was sentenced to three to 10 years in the state penitentiary.

Most itinerants lived a hardscrabble existence, taking few worldly goods with them as they traveled from place to place, and often doing odd jobs on the side to pay for their meals: The people who gathered for their sermons were often as poor as they were.

Traveling evangelists take a break beside their wagon on the road between Scott and Lafayette, La. By the time this photo was taken in October of 1938, the couple had spent 25 years on road, sharpening knives to meet expenses. Lettering on their wagon reads, "Repent. Ye shall all perish. Jesus is coming soon." *Lee Russell, Library of Congress*

A 1929 article in the *Knoxville News-Sentinel* told the story of a 74-year-old itinerant preacher who had collected too few pennies while evangelizing on street corners to pay for shelter. Winter weather drove him to the local jail for the night, where he was able to "stretch his aching bones on the concrete floor by the stove."

Other traveling preachers found more success.

Aimee Semple McPherson, a former atheist who made a name for herself debating Christians, did an about-face and embraced the faith at a tent revival. She also fell in love with the preacher — whom she soon married — and became a preacher herself. At just 19 years of age, she delivered a message before a crowd of 15,000 people in London.

She would later purchase a tent and hit the road in a 1912 Packard touring car, which she transformed into a "Gospel Car": It bore the message "Where will you spend eternity?" on one side and "Jesus is coming soon, get ready" on the other. McPherson filled it with Bibles and tracts and embarked on a trip down the East Coast and through the South, from Maine to Florida.

A religious tent picnic on the highway to Camp Blanding in Starke, Fla., urges visitors to "hurry back" and isn't afraid of a little product placement: in this case for Coca-Cola. Photo from December 1940. *Marion Post Wolcott, Library of Congress*

"I've never seen such grit," her mother said. "She was almost too weak to drive at the time, but she put on tires, cleaned the car, pounded the stakes for the tent, and put it up and took it down herself. The lord himself must have given her the strength to do all that."

McPherson, who would go on to found the Church of the Foursquare Gospel, was hardly the only preacher to pitch a tent beside the highway.

In fact, tent revivals began in the early 19th century as a way of spreading the word of God in rural frontier areas that lacked established churches, such as Kentucky and Ohio.

The first of these revivals, sometimes called camp meetings, took place at Gaspar River Church in southwestern Kentucky in the summer of 1800, and a larger one the next year drew between 10,000 and 25,000 people to Cane Ridge, Kentucky, northeast of Lexington. (State Route 537 retains the name Cane Ridge Road.) The meeting was a cooperative affair, featuring ministers from the Methodist, Baptist, and Presbyterian churches.

Some of the meetings were held in tents; others alongside brush arbors, temporary open-sided structures with a roof of brush, hay, or cut branches supported by vertical posts.

Over time, these revivals became a staple of the summer season, and nowhere more than in the South, where "hellfire-and-brimstone" preachers would call sinners to repentance and backsliders to recommit their lives to Jesus.

Their message of fear and hope resonated with local residents, who turned out in droves. The meetings provided them with a break from the despair of their daily lives, reaffirming their confidence in a better life to come in the hereafter.

In May of 1885, the *Memphis Avalanche* reported: "Though it was pouring rain at 6 o'clock this morning, the gospel tent held 1500 people when services began. Interest grows daily, and to get good seats many arrive two or three hours before the appointed time for service." A month later the newspaper in Anderson, South Carolina, noted that 8,000 people were packed "in and around the tent" on the final night of a three-week tent revival, which saw a total of 2,000 conversions.

The popularity of tent meetings only grew from there, finally peaking in the 1950s, as Americans hit the highways following the end of World War II. North Carolina native Billy Graham came to national attention in the fall of 1949 when he held a series of tent revival meetings in Hollywood, California. More than 1,000 churches supported him in the effort, which featured 58 services and drew more than 250,000 people. In the years that followed, Graham would transform the traditional tent revival into a series of "crusades" that filled football stadiums across the country.

Seeking a Sign

When there weren't preachers to spread the gospel, Southerners weren't shy about putting up signs by the side of the road to show the way.

And they still aren't.

Even today, you can find a multitude of signs along the highways of the South, some pointing the way to nearby churches, others calling for repentance. Some are impossible to miss: Towering billboards bear messages ranging from scriptures to the plea, "Forgive my sins Jesus. Save my soul."

Above: Religious signs like this one could be seen every mile, or even more frequently, along the Columbus-Augusta highway in December 1940.

Right: Billboards on the side of a building in New Orleans the following month advertise Catholic Masses, sandwiched around an ad for Oldsmobile.
Marion Post Wolcott, Library of Congress

Top: A sign for the Dillon Congregational Holiness Church in Dillon, S.C., on State Route 57, February, 2021. **Above:** Along Virginia State Route 220 south of Rocky Mount, February, 2021. *Author photos*

Top: Sign on a rural road in North Carolina in 2020. *Author photo*
Above: Between Columbus and Augusta, Georgia, December, 1940. *Marion Post Wolcott, Library of Congress*

Billboards seen in February 2021 on U.S. Highway 220, above, and U.S. Route 401 in North Carolina proclaim Jesus as the source of peace and "the answer to all your problems." *Author photos*

LaVarian Schrandt, above, stands by a sign in Hondo, Texas, that uses the Almighty as incentive to drive safely in a 1941 photo by Robert Schrandt. The message was reproduced on a more modern sign, on U.S. 90, prompting objections from non-Christians arguing for the separation of church and state.

The godfather of the roadside sign was a Kentucky coal miner named Henry Harrison Mayes, who felt God had saved him from a mining accident. In response, he decided to start setting up signs by the roadside to share the gospel with motorists on the highways of Appalachia.

It all started in 1917, and although many of his signs are gone now, having fallen victim to vandals and road-widening projects, a few may still be seen, such as one on Highway 411 near Benton, and another one north of Decatur, both in Tennessee.

Mayes' first instinct was to try preaching or even singing, but his voice wasn't cut out for either, so he turned to the written word. He painted messages on the side of coal train cars — a practiced frowned upon by the railroad — and even painted one on the side of a sow that was wandering around the mining camp in Middlesboro, Kentucky. (Mayes didn't quit his day job: He worked full time at the Fork Ridge Coal Company for 43 years).

But he really left his mark with the road signs, which were made of sturdy stuff. He started off using metal before he switched to concrete, which he poured into wooden molds he'd made by hand. Then he'd go out and dig holes on land beside the highway, not bothering to ask the owners' permission, and stand them up. A lot of them weren't any happier about it than the railroad company.

"I'm the most wanted man in America," he crowed. "The AAU has been after me for 45 years, the highway departments, too." (He was likely referring to the American Atheists' Union, not the better-known Amateur Athletic Union.) "The last time I heard from New York, they wanted $43 for the cost of removing two signs. I suppose I could go to jail for a million years."

The funny thing was, Mayes never learned to drive. He relied on friends to take him out in a truck along the highway to post the signs a couple of times a year.

And he *needed* a truck to transport them, because they weren't small: A photo of Mayes standing beside some shows them to be more than half again as tall as he was. Some were shaped like a cross, naturally, and others in the shape of a heart. They bore messages like "Jesus is Coming Soon," "Prepare to Meet God," and "Get Right With God." One was a bit more confrontational: "If You Go to Hell, It's Your Fault."

A newspaper columnist called him "the Johnny Appleseed of good words."

As of 1975, Mayes had lost count of how many signs he'd put up, but he claimed to have planted them in "at least 50 states and 82 foreign lands." And he had plans to travel from Georgia to Maine, then across the Midwest to Yellowstone Park, putting up 200 of them weighing 1,400 pounds apiece.

"I plan to have four of them outside each capital by 19 and 90, if there is a 19 and 90."

Unfortunately for Mayes, he didn't live that long. He died in 1986 with some crosses still in his possession, waiting for places to put them — and not necessarily on Earth. Some of the signs he left behind were accompanied by detailed instructions on how they should be erected in the heavens: specifically, the moon, or even Saturn.

"Everybody in the universe is under God," Mayes reasoned, "and maybe the people on Mars need a little prodding, too. ... Can you see it? Right in a crater, translated, 'Get Right With God.'"

A probe called Perseverance landed on Mars in February of 2021 and started to look around. So far, there's no sign of any highways, and Mayes' signs haven't made it to the Red Planet. Yet.

Left: A massive cross outside a church beside U.S. Highway 220 near Fieldale, Va., is impossible to miss.

Below: One of Henry Harrison Mayes' surviving markers, on U.S. 70 near Mebane, N.C. *Author photos*

A crowd gathers to hear a street evangelist meeting in front of a Kentucky saloon in 1906 or 1908. Religious opposition, especially among Southern Baptists, played a big part in the temperance movement that eventually led to Prohibition. *J.C. Lay, Library of Congress*

Drinking and Driving

Roadside sign south of Bardstown, Ky., possibly on U.S. 31E, directs drivers to a liquor dispensary ahead in 1940. *Marion Post Wolcott, Library of Congress*

Road to Perdition

Perhaps the most famous road associated with liquor really exists, even if the story that made it famous is a bit of lyrical fiction. John Lee Pettimore, the narrator of Steve Earle's 1988 tune, may not be a real person, but Copperhead Road is a real place. They just don't call it that anymore. When the song became a hit, too many people started stealing the road signs, they changed the name of the road near Mountain City, Tennessee, to Copperhead *Hollow* Road.

Fictional or not, it pays tribute to a very real period in American history that was bookended by two constitutional amendments, the second of which repealed the first — the only one ever to do so. But it would be a mistake to think that the nearly 15-year failed experiment that banned alcohol nationwide existed in isolation, even if the backwoods stills that created the alcohol did.

Even today, 33 states allow local cities or counties to go "dry" by banning the sale (or sometimes even the possession) of liquor. Large numbers of local jurisdictions have done just that in Arkansas and Kentucky, while Tennessee and Mississippi are dry by default: Counties can choose to allow alcohol, but they must specifically authorize it.

Liquor stores line U.S. 41E in Guthrie, Ky., just across the Tennessee state line in July 1940. "Immediately on entering state of Kentucky the greater increased number of liquor signs is very noticeable," photographer Marion Post Wolcott wrote. *Library of Congress*

Shortly after the end of Prohibition, drivers crossing into "wet" Kentucky counties from dry Tennessee were greeted almost immediately with liquor stores, just as California motorists find casinos clustered at the Nevada state line.

Oklahoma didn't repeal Prohibition until 1959, and Mississippi didn't repeal it until 1966. Many states held to "blue laws" that banned the sale of alcohol on Sundays, although 16 states repealed such laws in 2002. Virginia, Alabama, North Carolina, Mississippi, and West Virginia only allow the sale of hard liquor in state-owned "ABC stores" (for Alcohol Beverage Control).

A liquor dispensary near Bardstown, Ky., in July 1940. *Marion Post Wolcott, Library of Congress*

In some states, such as Alabama, Florida, Georgia, Louisiana, and Texas, liquor stores became known as "package stores," because liquor there must be sold in sealed bottles or packages when it leaves the store.

The Northside Package Store in Tallahassee, Fla, is seen in 1960. *Florida State Archives*

If Prohibition didn't end with the stroke of a pen in 1933, it didn't happen overnight, either. Statewide bans on alcohol had been tried as early as 1851 in Maine, but they usually didn't last. As they would in the 1920s, moonshine stills began to pop up around the state, and Maine eventually repealed its state prohibition in 1858, but that was hardly the end of the matter. In the second half of the 19th century, a number of women's groups, such as the Women's Christian Temperance Union, began to push for alcohol bans.

Carrie Nation, whose first husband had been an alcoholic, led a crusade to enforce Kansas' status as a dry state by any means necessary: She was arrested 30 times for attacking saloons, bars, and pharmacies (which sold liquor as "medicine"), using hammers and axes to smash up bottles and shelves in what she called "hatchetations." She claimed divine sanction for her actions, describing herself as "a bulldog running along at the feet of Jesus, barking at what he doesn't like."

But the women who opposed the sale of liquor for moral reasons weren't alone. They were joined in the fight by a group called the Anti-Saloon League, a group allied with the Ku Klux Klan that blamed the scourge of alcohol largely on Blacks.

"I would not say every Anti-Saloon Leaguer is a Ku Kluxer," said Clarence Darrow in 1924, the year before he achieved lasting fame as the defense lawyer in the Scopes evolution trial, "but every Ku Kluxer is an Anti-Saloon Leaguer."

It's no coincidence that the KKK would see its ranks swell into the millions during Prohibition, when the racist group branded itself as a private army bent on enforcing the liquor ban — against Blacks, Jews, Catholics, and immigrants.

The touchstone for it all came in the fall of 1906, when violence broke out in Atlanta following reports that four white women had been raped by Black men. The reports weren't confirmed, but they were enough to light the fuse on the powder keg of racism.

When newspapers linked the alleged rapes to Black-owned saloons on Decatur Street, white mobs responded.

As the *Fort Worth Telegram* reported:

"Ten dead negroes and probably half a hundred suffering from more or less serious wounds are the result of lynch fever which seized upon the white people of Atlanta tonight. ... As soon as the assaults (on the women) were announced by the night (newspaper) extras, the cry of "kill the negroes was heard in every section of the city and the deadly work began.

HIGHWAYS OF THE SOUTH

"There was not one great mob, but scores of small mobs made up of young men and half-grown boys, operating against the negroes in various sections of the city. Whenever a negro was seen he was immediately the target for bullets, knives, sticks, stones and every other weapon obtainable. Several of the negroes were literally beaten to death."

Most of the victims, the newspaper said, were pulled off streetcars and killed or severely beaten. Mobs invaded barbershops, attacked Black barbers and shoeshiners, and smashed up Black-owned saloons. *The Telegram* attributed that the rage to a dozen assaults on white women in two months, which "put whites in such a state of mind that the question of negro innocence was not considered."

By the time it was over, at least 25 Black people were killed.

The riots set off a chain reaction against liquor in the South, as state after state banned the sale of alcohol. By 1913, nine states were dry, many of them in the South. Oklahoma banned alcohol in 1907, with Georgia and Mississippi following suit the following year, and North Carolina and Tennessee adding themselves to the list in '09. The movement picked up steam in the teens, with West Virginia going dry in 1914, South Carolina and Alabama the next year, and a Virginia and Arkansas in 1916.

By that time, nearly half the nation — 23 states — was dry, with 17 states adopting prohibitions by direct vote. Building on that momentum, they said alcohol was hindering the nation's war effort, arguing that the barley used in brewing beer could be put to better use in making bread for American soldiers fighting the Germans overseas. And Germans were known for several things, not the least of which was brewing beer. Wisconsin's former lieutenant governor, John Strange, would have no doubt cringed at modern Oktoberfest celebrations held in many cities across the country. "We have German enemies across the water," he said. "We have German enemies in this country, too. And the worst of all our German enemies, the most treacherous, the most menacing, are Pabst, Schlitz, Blast, and Miller."

The 18th Amendment established Prohibition in January of 1919, and took effect a year later. By that time, only three states opposed it — New Jersey, Connecticut, and Rhode Island — with New Jersey ratifying it three years later. But the same problems that had plagued Maine's effort to go dry decades earlier soon re-emerged: moonshine makers and a thriving black market. Except this time, there was a twist. There hadn't been an effective method of distribution in the 1850s, but now there was.

Prohibition took effect just as the automobile had begun to gain traction on improving roads and highways that would become the battleground for the war between the rum runners and the "G-men" intent on stopping them.

Who was winning the battle?

Some statistics tell the story.

In 1920 alone, the feds seized more than 50 million drinks of whiskey, enough to give one to every male in the United States. That was $10 million worth of illegal alcohol, but no matter how much the government impounded, still more was being made and sold.

Between 1921 and 1925 government agents confiscated nearly 700,000 stills. This led "dry czar" Lincoln Andrews to tell acknowledge that "it means a great many people are distilling."

Julian Codman, a lawyer who opposed Prohibition, pressed him in an appearance before a Senate Judiciary subcommittee: "These figures show only a small part of the stills you can

Prohibition Administrator Ames Woodcock, left, and H.M. Lucious, secretary of the Maryland auto club, show off the Bureau of Prohibition's new insignia in 1925. *Library of Congress*

apprehend? There must be a great many more you don't know anything about."

Andrews admitted that "there must be some," while claiming that "a fair percentage" of stills were captured. But even if the figure of 696,933 was accurate, that amounted to roughly one still for every 164 citizens nationwide. It was also greater than the population of all but eight U.S. cities at the time: more stills than there were residents of Los Angeles, San Francisco, Washington, or New Orleans at the time. (Andrews thought the situation might improve if the government got into the business of selling beer, albeit not at bars or saloons.)

An illustration on the January 15, 1908 cover of Puck magazine shows prohibitionists "Marching Through Georgia." Barrels and banners bear messages like "vegetable tonic," "Water Wagon No. 1," "W.C.T.U." (Women's Christian Temperance Union), "Carrie Nation Cadets," and "The Lips that Touch Corn Likker Shall Never Touch Our Own." A woman with an axe may represent Nation herself. Georgia banned alcohol that same year. *Library of Congress*

Clockwise from top: Authorities pull barrels of liquor out of the cellar in Washington, D.C., in 1923; men pour confiscated whiskey into a sewer; a confiscated still was photographed at the Treasury Department during Prohibition.
Library of Congress

In 1923, a Prohibition agent went undercover to see how hard it was to buy alcohol in various American cities. It was relatively difficult in Washington, D.C., where he needed 2 hours and 8 minutes to make a purchase. But it was much easier elsewhere in the South. It took him just 21 minutes in St. Louis, 17 minutes in Atlanta, and a lightning-quick 35 seconds in New Orleans, which earned a reputation as a "the wettest city in the U.S." in a 1926 government poll.

Whiskey and champagne entered the Louisiana port city by ship from the Caribbean and transformed it into a "giant warehouse liquor store." Inland swamps, meanwhile, gave rum runners ample cover for their operations, as tiny Leonville, with fewer than 400 people, became a "the mecca of moonshine," attracting buyers from the neighboring state of Mississippi.

A mural outside a modern shop in Rocky Mount, Va., pays tribute in 2021 to Franklin County's moonshine history. *Author photo*

If the swamps and bayous of Louisiana gave still operators good cover, the hills of Appalachia and the Blue Ridge Mountains offered the same kind of haven in Virginia, West Virginia, and the Carolinas. During a 1920 raid in Whitley County, Kentucky, just north of the Tennessee state line, a dozen revenue agents looking for a still were forced to scramble around "the crookedest stream in the world" and through "a rough hollow," where they "had to climb over boulders and hang onto trees to get to the still." Then they had to hike two miles farther to get to another still. When all was said and done, they'd destroyed eight stills defended by armed moonshiners who fired at them numerous times (though none of the agents was hit).

How well were these stills hidden?

So well that a still hunter commented in 2012 that "you can literally walk up any creek" in Virginia's Franklin County "and find an old moonshine still."

He continued: "I decided to put that bold statement to the test one day: I drove around Franklin County, randomly picked a creek, parked on the side of the road, and just walked up the creek. And I found three moonshine stills."

It's no wonder.

During Prohibition, Franklin County earned a reputation as the Moonshine Capital of the World, and FBI Director J. Edgar Hoover once referred to it as "the wettest place on earth."

You needed raw material to make moonshine, and literally tons of malt, yeast, rye, corn meal, and sugar poured into Franklin County. During one four-year span, nearly 34 million pounds of sugar were sold in Franklin County — more than 350 pounds for every one of its 24,000 residents, 99 percent of whom were involved in the moonshine trade.

One of those residents, a certain Mrs. Sharpe, said she'd moved more than 220,000 gallons of whiskey out of the county.

Bootleggers (so named because they hid bottles of booze in their boots) did what they could to keep their moonshine out of sight. It didn't take long before lawmen realized they could spot a rum runner by listening for the gurgling sound in the back of vehicles that rumbled along bumpy country roads. But the lawbreakers responded by coming up with non-gurgling cans that hid the sound. Over a four-year period, they imported 600,000 five-gallon "quiet cans" via boxcar into Franklin County alone.

A lot of those boxcars were unloaded in Boones Mill — named not for Daniel Boone but for mill operator Jacob Boon. The town never had a population of more than 400 people, but it was located on a rail line at an important crossroads of what would become U.S. Highway 220 and State Route 684.

Road-improvement efforts helped the bootleggers, too. The more roads were paved, the smoother their getaway path, especially in North Carolina, where good roads were a priority.

The Boones Mill depot, photographed in February 2021. *Author photo*

Bootleggers developed other tactics on the road, as well. *The Richmond Times-Dispatch* reported that drivers transporting moonshine had begun to employ "naval techniques" against law enforcement. They'd travel in convoys, using a large car to delay pursuing officers while speedier bootleg cars made their escape.

As an example, the paper cited an incident in Martinsville, a city just across the North Carolina state line in Virginia that later became home to a NASCAR speedway: "Officers on Wednesday night saw two suspicious cars headed for Patrick (County). They waylaid the cars a few miles beyond Martinsville, expecting the machines to return. They did, a small car with a heavy load being followed by a seven-passenger machine of powerful build. The little car went by like a flash, and when the officers put in chase, the heavier car maneuvered to keep the road (clear) and blocked all efforts of the Henry County officers to get by."

In the end, however, the pursuing officers caught up to their prey when the large blockade car pulled too wide at a curve, allowing officers to fly past — in much the same way stock-car drivers pass on the inside when the car ahead of them rides up high on a curve.

One clever North Carolina man played a different game of chicken with authorities: He decided to hide his booze in eggs, of all things. He would use a sharp instrument to poke a hole in the small end of the egg; then he'd suck out its contents and replace them with whiskey before sealing the opening with a little plaster of Paris and selling them at "very fancy prices," according to *The Charlotte News*.

"Eggs thus treated found ready buyers at $4 a dozen," the newspaper reported, "and detection was difficult, until one inebriate customer let one of the loaded eggs drop to the floor." The sheriff chased him "all over this county as far as Winston-Salem" for several days, before finally arresting him at a pool hall.

Even though Southern states had embraced Prohibition early on, it was a decision they soon came to regret. The loss of liquor sales meant a loss of sales tax revenues, with still operators now selling direct to the public. According to one estimate, Franklin County still operators sold so much whiskey they would have paid $5.5 million in excise taxes at the 1920 rate if the liquor had been sold legally. Meanwhile, the region's pious opposition to "the devil's brew" was balanced by a lingering sense of rebellion from the Civil War era: The federal government had no business telling sons of the South what they should and shouldn't do.

"I just don't see that the government has a right to regulate what a man does with his own corn," one Franklin County resident said.

That's probably one reason moonshiners continued to operate illegal stills long after the end of Prohibition. The largest still ever found in Franklin County was destroyed in the 1970s, one of about 300 discovered there between 1960 and 1985.

The Checkered Flag

Prohibition and bootlegging left another legacy, too: NASCAR.

When Prohibition was repealed, the need for moonshiners to outrun the law wasn't as pressing, but their love of speed remained. So some of them started meeting up at fairgrounds and local tracks, where they'd race in front of fans. They'd take their whiskey cars and paint numbers on the side, then head down to Lakewood Speedway in Atlanta, (later described in the *Atlanta Constitution* as "the house that whisky built") or another Southern track.

Raymond Parks was 14 when he ran away from his home in the Georgia mountains. It was 1928 when he started working for a local moonshiner, and it wasn't long before he started making a killing. He invested the money he earned working a still and delivering whiskey in services stations and the racing. In 1938, he formed a racing team that consisted of two cousins — who were also moonshine runners — and a mechanic known for working on bootleggers' cars.

One of the cousins, Lightnin' Lloyd Seay, won the first major stock car race at Lakewood that same year, with 20,000 fans in attendance. He was just 18 at the time.

In 1941, he won again at Lakewood, starting behind the rest of the field but working his way up to win the $450 prize from Bob Flock — another bootlegger who went by aliases like "Frankie Johns" and "Robert Clark." It was Seay's third win in just two weeks, following victories at Daytona and High Point, N.C. But he didn't race again. He died the following day at his brother's house, when a cousin showed up to settle a dispute over the sugar used to make the family's moonshine. The cousin shot him in the stomach.

That same year, Parks' other cousin, Roy Hall, won the national stock car title. But Hall's connection to bootlegging came back to haunt him in 1945, when police banned him, Flock, and three other racers — one-third of the field — from driving in the Labor Day race at Lakewood because they'd been convicted of transporting liquor. Hall had been arrested 16 times, dating back to 1938. He'd also been sentenced a month earlier to a year in prison for taking part in a "bootlegger sweepstakes" event in which a driver had died on the Buford Highway, otherwise known as State Route 13, northeast of Atlanta.

Records showed that Hall paid $300 fines in three different Georgia counties for violating liquor laws in 1939. But the 30,000 fans at the track that day didn't care: They wanted to see Hall race. With the crowd on the brink of getting out of control, police relented and let him compete. He ended up winning, but he went to prison anyway.

His troubles weren't over, either: He was also convicted of robbing a bank, which put him in prison for three more years after he completed his "bootlegger sweepstakes" sentence.

Flock, meanwhile, was arrested in the Labor Day race at Lakewood in 1947 after police "discovered him trying to sneak into a race." But the cops didn't get him right away.

His younger brother, Tim, would later recall that Flock tied a handkerchief around his face so police wouldn't know who he was. But a police captain recognized him and, when Flock peeled out to make his getaway, the captain sent a motorcycle cop to head him off. Flock went through the fence and took off, and the police couldn't catch him — although he did turn himself in a week later and paid a $140 fine.

Above: Racing at Daytona Beach, 1947.

Right: Red Byron, center, accepts the trophy for winning at Daytona that year. *Florida State Archives*

"I would have won that race if the cops had stayed out of it," Flock later said.

Drivers were still using 1938 or '39 Fords to race that year because they worked so well for running liquor. Tim Flock estimated that his family went through 100 of the cars, "because you could hollow them out and stack 180 gallons in there easy."

In 1947, driver Bill France founded the National Championship Stock Car Circuit, a series of races to begin in January at Daytona Beach. This wasn't the modern Daytona International Speedway (which wouldn't be built until more than a decade later). It was a track right on the beach, where drivers had been competing since as far back as 1902.

HIGHWAYS OF THE SOUTH

Red Byron, driving for Raymond Parks' team, won that first race.

Fonty Flock, Bob's brother, won the season championship in '47, and the following year, France formed NASCAR, with Byron winning the first points championship.

Martinsville Speedway in southern Virginia opened in 1947, with Red Byron winning the 50-lap main event. It continues to host NASCAR events, such as this one in 2019. *Author photo*

Racing at Daytona in 1952. *Florida State Archives*

Two views of Copperhead Hollow Road, formerly known as Copperhead Road, referenced in Steve Earle's ode to moonshiners. The road's name was changed to prevent signs from being stolen, but a visit on a snowy Tuesday in mid-February 2021 found no signs in evidence. *Author photos*

Tobacco Road

What many have forgotten is that liquor wasn't the only vice that came under attack in the late 19th and early 20th centuries. Tobacco, too, was targeted, even as it grew more popular — and profitable — in the South.

Numerous place names and sights in the South, concentrated in Virginia and North Carolina, reflect the influence of the tobacco industry at the time. Two prominent cigarette brands took their names from Winston-Salem, North Carolina, while Virginia Slims branded the commonwealth's name.

And Duke University got its name when James Buchanan Duke, founder of the American Tobacco Company, donated $40 million to Trinity College in Durham, North Carolina.

A Lucky Strike smokestack stands alongside a water tower in downtown Reidsville, N.C., in 2020. *Author photo*

American Tobacco was the Standard Oil of big tobacco. Duke got wind of an automated cigarette-rolling machine that had been patented in 1881; obtaining a license shortly afterward, he used it to mass-produce the product for the first time. In 1890, he forced a takeover of four major competitors and founded the American Tobacco Company, which immediately controlled 90 percent of the market (although Bull Durham continued to compete with the slogan "Roll your own.")

Old Bull sign on the Bull Durham building in Durham, N.C., with a Lucky Strike water tower in the distance. *Author photo*

This virtual monopoly ran afoul of the Sherman Antitrust Act, and the Supreme Court ordered it broken up in 1911, on the same day it ruled that Standard Oil be dissolved. And the fast-growing cigarette industry attracted the ire of those who viewed the habit as disgusting and immoral.

The Women's Christian Temperance Union, although focused primarily on alcohol, denounced cigarettes, as well. So did prominent businessmen including Henry Ford and breakfast cereal mogul Harvey Kellogg. Lucy Page Gaston, a former WCTU member, formed the Anti-Cigarette League in 1899. Much like the Anti-Saloon League, it pushed for full prohibition on smoking, and Gaston did her best to link the two movements, promising that temperance workers could do "no greater service at this junction than to join hands enthusiastically in a greater national movement of (banning) the cigarette."

Camel Cigarettes were made in North Carolina, but this smoke-blowing sign, proclaiming "I'd walk a mile for a Camel," was a fixture in New York's Times Square. Here, it's seen in 1948. *William van de Poll, Wikimedia Commons*

"Souls will be saved from eternal ruin, homes will be saved from untold sorrow, and our nation will be saved by its noble sons."

Gaston received enthusiastic support from the YMCA, which noted that smoking could be hazardous to your health decades before the surgeon general reached the same conclusion. It warned that smoking cigarettes could cause a "lack of robustness, anemic appearance, imperfect development, brazen attitudes, (and) listless actions."

And the YMCA wasn't alone. Two years after the league's formation, it boasted a membership of 300,000, and by 1909, a total of 13 states — including Arkansas, Oklahoma, and Tennessee — had banned smoking.

Even where outright bans weren't passed, condemnation was widespread. The minutes from a 1906 meeting of the Annual Assembly of the Churches of East Tennessee, North Georgia, and Western North Carolina contained the following censure:

"After due consideration this assembly agrees to stand, with one accord, in opposition to the use of tobacco in any form. It is offensive to those who do not use it; weakens and impairs the nervous system; is a near relative to drunkenness; bad influence and example to the young; useless expense, the money for which ought to be used to clothe the poor, spread the gospel or make the homes of our country more comfortable; and last we believe its use to be contrary to the teaching of Scripture, and as Christ is our example we cannot believe that He would use it in any form or under any circumstances."

But every state ban was repealed at the height of liquor Prohibition. The reason was simple: World War I created a demand for cigarettes among U.S. soldiers overseas, and it was considered unpatriotic to deny them this simple pleasure. The YMCA, which had previously condemned smoking, actually started collecting cigarettes to be sent to the troops (although its primary concern, a prohibition on selling cigarettes to minors, remained in effect).

The South Divided

The Henry County Courthouse in Martinsville, Va., features a war memorial obelisk, seen here, as well as a Civil War Confederate memorial (not pictured). *Author photo*

Pride and Prejudice

In some ways, the modern South is still bound the Confederacy and the Civil War fought over slavery 150 years ago.

Yet in others, it's more integrated than the place I called home for most of my life. A California native, I moved to Virginia in the summer of 2018. But my hometown on the West Coast practiced redlining (housing discrimination) so persistently in the first half of the 20th century that neighborhoods remained segregated in the 21st.

Out here in Virginia, though, I live in an integrated suburban neighborhood where everyone greets you with a friendly "hello" regardless of the color of your skin.

There's still racism here, though, deep-seated and hard to extricate for the fiber of the place. The culture of the region was so intertwined with the racist class structure of the antebellum South that separating the two, at least in the minds of some, is a challenge to say the least.

Is "Southern Pride" an expression of regional identity or an echo of racial prejudice?

Th answer depends on who you ask.

Civil War monuments to the "heroes" who fought for the South during the Civil War sit in front on many Southern courthouses, placed there by the United Daughters of the Confederacy, which was established in 1894 and also funded the construction of a monument to the Ku Klux Klan in 1926.

You still see Confederate battle flags flying by the roadside in some places, many of them on back roads that are off the beaten path, but some alongside highways and major thoroughfares. And some of those highways themselves bear names of men who led the South in that war over slavery.

It's been so long that generations have come and gone. Some remain steeped in the residue of that conflict, while others are all but oblivious to its lingering effects. And this raises uncomfortable questions: What happens when shrines to a long-ago era become objects of nostalgia in their own right? What does that say about their purpose and meaning? Some born in the 20th century have fond memories of the Lee Highway, yet may not know or care that it honors a Confederate general. The associate the name instead with childhood road trips in the backseat of their parents' car or outings at the bowling alleys, skating rinks, and drive-in theaters that once stood alongside them. Fond memories, not echoes of hatred.

Yet such names also give comfort to those who cling to prejudices from long ago, who are well aware of the original connection — and they feel like a slap in the face to the descendants of those exploited and brutalized by slavery and its aftermath. Jim Crow is a far more recent injustice, and racial inequality is anything but a thing of the past.

It hasn't been that long since Black travelers had to stay in separate hotels along the highways, enter theaters through separate entrances, and stay away from "whites only" lunch counters and water fountains. Segregation wasn't just visible in the South, it was the rule: a way of life.

Two photos by Jack Delano from 1941 show the contrast at the bus station in Durham, N.C. *Library of Congress*

Right: A sign for a now-defunct roadside store called Little Rebel still stands on U.S. 220 in Summerfield, N.C.

Below: Several car washes under the name Southern Pride can be seen in Virginia. This one is just off U.S. 220 in Martinsville. *Author photos*

Left: A monument dedicated by the United Daughters of the Confederacy "to the memory of the Confederate dead of Franklin County," sits outside the courthouse of this Virginia town off U.S. Business Route 220 in 2021.

Below: A Confederate flag is displayed on a roadside stand in Boones Mill, Va., on U.S. 220 in 2021. *Author photos*

Trail of Tears

The history of racial brutality in the South dates back before Jim Crow and before the Civil War, and it extended well beyond free people brought as slaves from Africa and the families they raised here.

Indigenous peoples were victims, too, as the slaves who were being brought in worked land that belonged to the Cherokee, Creek, Seminole, Choctaw, and Chickasaw nations — before the U.S. government took it from them by force. Then they marched them on foot, over what one Choctaw leader called a "trail of tears and death" to a new "Indian Territory" in the West.

The Trail of Tears wasn't a single path, but a number of different paths west that covered some 5,045 miles over eight states in the South and the southern tip of Illinois.

A British proclamation in 1763 had set aside the region from the Appalachian range to the Mississippi River as a protected area for indigenous peoples, but U.S. independence had rendered that proclamation moot. Even before the revolution, Daniel Boone had pushed across the Appalachians and into Kentucky, which would become a state in 1792. (The very name "Kentucky" stems, ironically, from an Iroquois word meaning "on the meadow" or "prairie," proof enough that the land lay beyond the mountains.)

But it wasn't until 1829, when gold was discovered on Cherokee land in Georgia, that the issue became pressing to white settlers. With mines turning out 300 ounces of gold a day, land speculators began to petition the government to take control of indigenous lands. And a year later, in 1830, Andrew Jackson signed the Indian Removal Act, empowering the president to negotiate with the nations for their removal and relocation to land west of the Mississippi.

It wasn't just about gold, though: The "five civilized tribes," as they became known, had already accepted many European customs, some learning to speak English, converting to Christianity, and embracing a system of land ownership and farming. But those farms provided white Southerners with something more to covet: fertile land that had already been prepared for them. All they had to do was take it — which is exactly what they did.

While Jackson acted on legislation at the federal level, states passed laws that limited native land rights.

The Supreme Court struck down those laws in 1832, affirming the sovereignty of indigenous nations, "in which the laws of Georgia (and other states) can have no force."

It didn't matter.

Jackson scoffed at the ruling, saying that if there was no one to enforce the decision, it wouldn't matter — and he himself had no intention of enforcing it.

The Choctaw and Chickasaw nations both signed agreements to vacate their land in 1830. that same year, with the Creek following in 1832. The Cherokee were the ones who fought back in court, and won that Supreme Court ruling, but wound up being "escorted" off their land anyway. The Seminoles also resisted, and many succeeded in retaining some of their land in Florida.

But many Cherokee who stood their ground were forced from their homes at gunpoint. Then they were housed in internment camps for weeks, and made to march long distances or (in one case) travel by boat over the Tennessee, Ohio, Mississippi, and Arkansas rivers.

Though the Indian Removal Act had allotted $500,000 for compensation and transportation, most of that money got lost in a bureaucratic shuffle, meaning supplies for these journeys were nonexistent. Hunger and disease were rampant, adding to the inevitable exhaustion of traveling such long distances on foot.

John Bell led 660 Cherokee over this trail from Fort Cass in southeastern Tennessee to Evansville, Ark., just west of Oklahoma, in October 1938. This sign marks a spot on the trail in Pulaski, Tenn. *Author photo*

Nearly one-third of the Cherokee — 4,000 of 15,000 involved in the "relocation" — perished in the process, although 1,000 of them were able to build new homes in North Carolina.

Those who survived wound up in Indian Territory, but they didn't get to keep that, either. As white settlers continued to push westward, they claimed the land there, just as they had taken the soil beyond the Appalachians and in the Deep South as their own. In 1907, Indian Territory ceased to exist. In its place, the state of Oklahoma joined the union.

Jim Crow

When Georgia embarked on an ambitious road project in 1890s, it didn't pay workers to build these new thoroughfares. Slavery had been abolished, but there was a loophole in the Thirteenth Amendment, which banned involuntary servitude "except as punishment for a crime."

In this loophole, business owners saw an opportunity: If they accused a Black man of a crime and convinced a white jury to go along with the trumped-up charges — hardly a difficult task a region infused with racism — they could step in and pay any court fees or fines. In exchange, however, the accused would have to sign a contract agreeing to work off the debt without receiving any pay. They might do so by working the fields, digging ditches, or performing menial tasks for merchants. Or they might lease their forced workers out to coal mines and other industries for a profit.

Convict laborers working on a road in Oglethorpe County, Ga., in 1941. The practice of using chain gangs on highways wasn't abolished in the South until the 1950s. *Jack Delano, Library of Congress*

It was easy for unscrupulous white business owners to claim the debt had never been repaid, keeping workers bound to them indefinitely. And because many Southern states didn't accept the testimony of African Americans in court, they had no way to challenge the lies that kept them in servitude.

This practice was eventually abolished, only to be replaced by something even more cruel: the chain gang. Under this "reform," the accused no longer worked for private business owners. Instead, the state put chains around their ankles, and bound them together to work, eat, and sleep in the open as they labored in the service of "civilization." Slavery had been abolished, but these chain gangs consisted almost entirely of Black men, many of whom had been found guilty by white juries of crimes they didn't commit. In fact, 90 percent of those incarcerated in Georgia were Black. It was slavery by another name, and it tasted just as bitter.

This practice continued for a century, and not just in Georgia but in many other Southern states, until it was finally abolished in the 1950s.

Still, that was hardly the end of the highway's impact on communities of color. Segregation remained in effect for African Americans, who had to find places where they'd be accepted or risk being shown the door, sometimes violently.

In 1936, a New York City postal carrier named Victor Hugo Green published his first *Negro Motorist Green Book* "to give the Negro traveler information that will keep him from running into difficulties, embarrassments and to make his trip more enjoyable." The book was published annually for three decades, through 1966, with 15,000 copies being printed each year. "It was one of the survival tools of the segregated life," Green said.

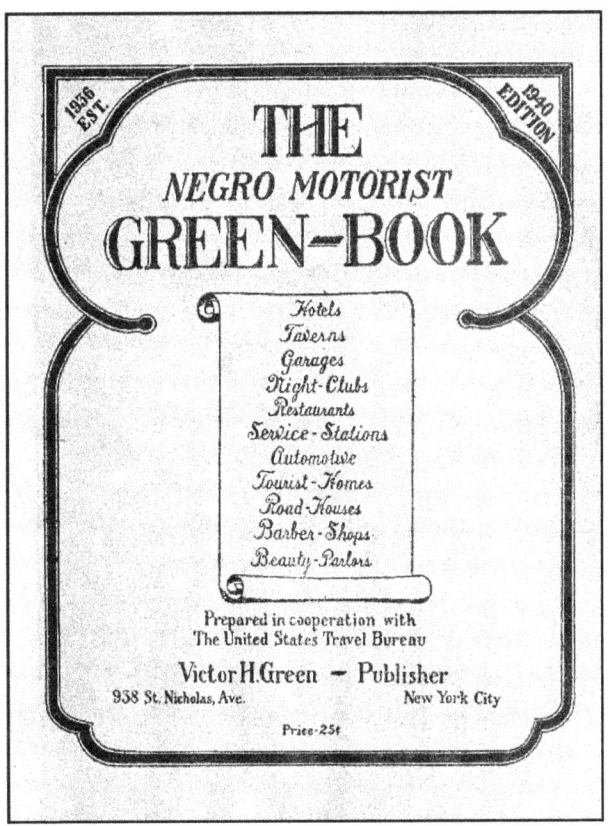

The 1940 edition of The Negro Motorist Green Book. *Smithsonian*

The guide went beyond hotels, gas stations, and restaurants to spotlight barbershops, churches, taverns, beauty salons, and mechanics. Its introduction began as follows:

"The idea of 'The Green Book' is to give the Motorist and Tourist a Guide not only of the Hotels and Tourist Homes in all of the large cities, but other classifications that will be found useful wherever he may be. Also facts and information that the Negro Motorist can use and depend upon."

Green invited his readers to contribute places that weren't in the book: "There are thousands of places that the public doesn't know about and aren't listed. Perhaps you know of some? If so send in their names and addresses and the kind of business, so that we might pass it along to the rest of your fellow Motorists."

The book served as the inspiration for the title of the 2018 film *Green Book*, which won the Academy Award for Best Picture.

A Tour of the South

Green stopped printing the book in 1966, two years after passage of the Civil Rights Act, but that didn't mean everything was perfect. Far from it. In '64, a *Tampa Bay Times* reporter named Samuel Adams wrote a seven-part series called "Highways of Hope," detailing the two weeks he spent on a 4,300-mile journey across the South. He visited a dozen states with his wife, Elenora and amid "heartening signs of progress" found a mixture of "open defiance, with violence just beneath the surface," along with evasion and subterfuge.

"Food and lodging can be found at a price in un-segregated facilities on main highways through much of the South," he wrote. "But the Negro tourist who strays from the busy thoroughfares almost anywhere south of the Mason-Dixon line may have trouble spending his money except in segregated restaurants and motels."

Adams found that some restaurants put "reserved" signs on tables as a way of denying service to people of color, while others closed up shop if they thought a Black patron was about to ask for service. A drive-in on U.S. 82 near Hinesville, Georgia, pulled this trick: A waitress announced "we're closing" when she saw the Adamses drive up at 3:30 in the afternoon, even though customers inside were being served.

Some motels and restaurants claimed — falsely — that they weren't able to provide the services they advertised. One drive-in even stated on its menus: "We reserve the right to change prices without notice." Adams noted in his account that "prices do double suddenly for Negro patrons." In Huntington, West Virginia, some establishments tried to get around the Civil Rights Act by calling themselves private clubs.

The Hotel Clark in Memphis offered "the best service" to "COLORED ONLY" in 1939. *Marion Post Wolcott, Library of Congress*

When the couple sought to rent a room at some motels, they were told that the only rooms left were for larger parties. Adams asked about the price, but the manager told him, "I'd better wait for a big family. There are some more motels right up the road." When it came to finding a restroom, some were labeled as out of order, and at a Gulf station in Greenwood, Mississippi, the person on duty claimed not to have a key.

When the Adamses got to Alabama, they were greeted by a series of signs. The first one anyone was likely to see along any major highway entering the state, Adams wrote, was a huge billboard that displayed the Confederate flag and a picture of segregationist governor George Wallace. The next sign read "Whites Only," and the one after that touted the highway construction program with the phrase "Your Tax Dollars at Work."

A printed message at one hotel promised that "every penny of Negro trade forced on this establishment will be donated to the White Citizens Council" — one of several groups by this name formed in the aftermath of the *Brown v. Board of Education* ruling to oppose racial integration in schools… and elsewhere.

In Louisiana, the Adamses had trouble getting a room outside New Orleans.

In Mississippi, they were warned not to:
- Travel on the highway after dark.
- Use the "white" restrooms at a particular gas station, because the attendant would alert police and have them arrested down the road on a bogus traffic charge.
- Stay out after midnight in Clarksdale.
- Get arrested on a traffic charge, or their vehicle would be impounded, Adams would be thrown in jail, and his wife would be "left on the street without transportation."

Even big-name entertainers like bandleader Duke Ellington were forced to stay at "colored" motels. Here, he and his band play baseball in front of the Astor Motel in Florida, 1955. *Charlotte Brooks, Library of Congress*

In his conclusion, Adams wrote that "fear rides with Negros who drive through the South. ... There is far less reason for a Negro to be afraid now. Yet fear remains, and some of our northern friends refuse to drive through the South to visit us."

As highways became freeways, they bypassed urban centers, putting the emerging middle class on a fast track to a new postwar haven in the suburbs. Downtowns, the palatial Emerald Cities of the railroad era, and were left behind, along with the low-income residents — many of them people of color — who couldn't afford to move out.

Rock 'n' roll pioneer Little Richard remembered: "Black people lived right by the railroad tracks, and the train would shake their houses at night. I would hear it as a boy, and I thought, I'm gonna make a song that sounds like that."

Left: A family with new Oldsmobile stops at a Mobil station in Washington, D.C., in April 1955. *Addison N. Scurlock, public domain*

Right: A sign at Lewis Mountain in Shenandoah National Park, Va., indicates a segregated area with a coffee shop, cottages, a campground, and picnic area in the Blue Ridge Mountains during the 1930s. *National Park Service*

Above: A backdoor entrance for people of color at the New Crescent Theatre on Hayden Street, Old U.S. 49W, in Belzoni, Miss., 1939.

Left: A sign for segregated tourist cabins at the Bronzeville Inn along a highway in South Carolina, 1939. *Marion Post Wolcott, Library of Congress*

HIGHWAYS OF THE SOUTH

Interstate 95 under construction in Miami. It was one of two new interstates that resulted in the demolition of much of the city's historic African-American Overtown neighborhoods. *Florida State Archives*

As more highways were built, poor neighborhoods at the core of these decaying inner cities came became "expendable," and were bulldozed to make way for President Eisenhower's interstate system. This was the fate of Miami's historic Overtown business district, described as "the commercial and cultural heart of Miami," which was demolished to create Interstate 95. Some 10,000 residents were displaced.

The same thing happened in North Nashville, where Interstate 40 was routed through the Black community, laying waste to businesses, more than 600 homes, and six Black churches. According to one estimate, more than a million people were displaced across the nation during the first two decades of interstate highway construction, even as activists decried the routing of "white highways through black bedrooms."

Two Worlds, Two Legacies

How does one reconcile this tragic history of hate and exploitation with the beauty of the tree-lined highways that are its legacy? Can we appreciate the roadways that bind us together while condemning the horrors of strife and division that made them possible?

In recognition of the pain inflicted upon too many Americans in our past, reminders of that pain are being removed from highways built in homage to the "lost cause" of the Civil War in the early 1900s. Auto trails honoring the likes of Confederate President Jefferson Davis and others are being renamed, and monuments to them are being removed; others, however, remain.

History challenges us to remember the good and the bad, but it's *how* we remember it that matters. The words "never forget" remind us that, if we're arrogant enough to dismiss the mistakes and malice in our past, we'll likely find ourselves repeating it. Yet if celebrate those things with monuments and proclamations, we magnify the harm already done.

As the pictures on these pages show, the effects of that hatred linger, and should not be forgotten, even as we marvel at the highways that both brought us together and tore us apart.

Part Two
Southern Comforts

At the Pump

The Airplane Service Station opened in 1930 along U.S. Highway 25 in Powell, north of Knoxville, and is on the national register of Historic Places. As of 2020, when this picture was taken, it was being used as a barber shop. *Author photo*

Full Tank, Will Travel

Once upon a time, you couldn't go more than a few miles without hitting a gas station. At the start of the 1920s, there were just 15,000 of them, but that number rose to 124,000 by 1929. They were at every intersection in town and beside every off-ramp.

The main reason there were so many is that they were needed. For one thing, the chances that you'd break down on the road were a lot higher. Gas was often dispensed, in the early days, at garages that could help you with a blown a tire or a radiator leak —

common occurrences back then. There was no such thing as self-service: Drivers could count on hearing the sound of a bell when they rolled into a station, signaling a friendly attendant to greet them with a smile and an offer to check the, oil, tires, wipers, radiator, and whatever else might need a look.

An abandoned garage and service station on U.S. 25E in Lily, Ky., north of Corbin. *Author photo*

Shell gas stations even spelled it out in a motto over the garages at every location: "Service Is Our Business."

In the early days, most cars were less than reliable, and the majority of roads were less than smooth. Most, in fact, were unpaved. So it's no wonder that an ode to the motorcar published by a Louisville newspaper in 1920 contained the following lines:

> *The car of honest poverty*
> *Though others scorn, you're dear to me*
> *Your every fender has a dent*
> *Your top looks like a life misspent*
> *Bills for repair now keep me broke*
> *I've put most everything in soak*
> *(But) though on homely fare we dine*
> *I still can say the car is mine*

It's no wonder that, by then, many newspapers were printing full pages of ads from auto repair shops, commonly known then as simply "garages."

At first, it was these garages that sold gas as just one of many services they offered. In 1920, R.D. Bond Tire & Supply in Chattanooga put it at the top of its newspaper ad, but also included a laundry list of products it offered, including two motor oil brands (Mobil and Havoline), and:

- Transmission oil
- Graphite grease
- Tube patches
- Horns
- Automobile soap
- Spark plugs
- Jacks
- Ford timers
- Chamois
- Sponges
- Blowout patches

It paid for garages to offer gas because, even if your car was running properly, you needed fuel more often back then. A Model T didn't get the kind of gas mileage a Prius does. In fact, the average car in 1923 got just 14 miles to the gallon.

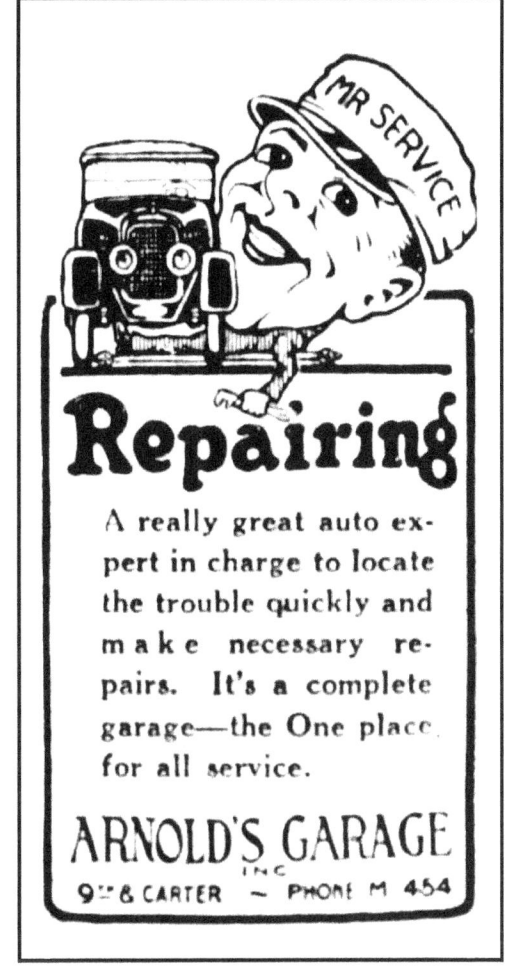

A January 1920 newspaper ad for a garage in Chattanooga, Tenn., called it "the One place for all service."

At the dawn of the 1920s, most garages and early service stations were still mom-and-pop operations, much as early motels were. But as branded gas stations took off, the situation reversed itself: Instead of a lot of garages selling gas, many gas stations started adding attached garages. It wasn't long before most standalone garages stopped selling gas, unable to compete with the new "service stations."

At first, many gas stations were just small sheds or cottages with pumps out front. These cottages — like those built by the Pure Oil Company — or house-style stations were designed to fit in with neighborhoods, proof of just how common cars were becoming in the 1920s, and how pervasive the need for gas was. It wasn't just being dispensed in downtown garages anymore, but in residential areas and at rural crossroads.

Top: Central Garage in Jacksonville, Fla., had a couple of gas pumps out front in the early 1900s. *Florida State Archives*

Above: An abandoned garage sits on North Carolina Highway 119 north of Mebane in 2021. *Author photo*

Top: Holley's Auto Repair & Parts on Bridge Street in Martinsville, Va., seen in 2021, is located near the center of town. *Author photo*

Above: A garage in Clearwater offered air and vulcanizing (a process for hardening tires) along with Buick sales and service nearly a century earlier, in May 1922. *Florida State Archives*

Two different examples of "house" type gas stations are seen in these two pictures.

Above: A log cabin station is preserved at Culver's on U.S. 31E in Nelson County, Ky.

Right: An old Pure Oil station on U.S. 70 in Durham, N.C., is maintained alongside a modern station. *Author photos*

Gas stations were once more common in city centers than they are today, as these photos of Cities Service stations taken in 1964 in Tallahassee (top) and in 1955 in Jacksonville illustrate. Cities Service rebranded itself as Citgo in the mid-1960s. *Florida State Archives*

Cottage-style stations fit well on downtown corners, where space was at a premium. They could be wedged into tight spaces in front of other buildings. In a more rural setting, they could fit on triangle-shaped lots between two diverging roads at a "Y" intersection — a premium location that was highly visible and easily accessible.

Top: A Pure station in Danville, Va., with two garage additions.

Left: A cottage-style station on a corner in Danville, Va.; a second building and a canopy were added later. *Author photos*

It wasn't long before the cottage/house concept expanded. Pure Oil added garage bays for repairs that looked like garages on an actual home, gabled to match the original peaked roof on the structure.

Top: As time passed, Pure abandoned the cottage-style station for a more modern, rectangular box style. *Florida State Archives*

Above: A newspaper ad for Woco Pep, short for Wofford Oil, an Alabama-based company that had a partnership with Pure. It also had a major presence in Southern states like Florida, Georgia, and Mississippi. Woco Pep declared itself "the King of Motor Fuel," and boasted in 1929 that it had 517 locations in Mississippi alone.

Even before the first "house" stations were built, in the early 1920s, some sites were adding canopies out front to shield attendants from the elements.

The popularity of cottage-style stations began to wane in the 1930s, as stations turned their attention away from residential neighborhoods and focused increasingly on major streets and highways.

Many of the cottage-style stations that remained added garages that were nothing more than flat-topped boxes. But more often than not, the older stations were torn down and replaced with a more functional (but less aesthetically pleasing) "icebox" model: a rectangle that consisted of an office on one side, with two or three adjacent service bays, and pumps out front, often covered by a canopy.

Most canopies were attached to the main structure of older stations and garages, but the newer iceboxes often had detached canopies out front.

A Texaco station with attached canopy on U.S. 50 in Winchester, Va., 1940. *Arthur Rothstein, Library of Congress*

Left: An old Sinclair station with a sturdy canopy sits on a stretch of rural road (Wentworth Street) west of Reidsville, N.C.

Above: A restored Sinclair service station from 1933 sits on Route 66 at the Paris Springs Junction in Missouri. *Author photos*

Two examples of the icebox style of service station. **Top:** An old Texaco station in Ewing, Va. **Above:** A station on U.S. 220 in Virginia. *Author photos*

An old Cities Service icebox station on The Great Road near Fieldale, Va. *Author photo*

As with any other business, attracting customers was top priority. Automotive pages in newspapers were full of ads touting how one company's fuel was better than all its competitors.

Billups Gasoline, founded in 1927 with two pumps (one for premium and one for Ethyl) at a station in Carrolton, Mississippi, grew into a chain of more than 600 service stations across a dozen states. The chain stretched from Delaware down the East Coast to Florida and across the Gulf Coast to Louisiana — with Missouri and Tennessee thrown in for good measure. Customers could "Fill up with Billups" at the "sign of the friendly hand."

Billups stations marketed various products to restless kids in the backseat, displaying everything from teddy bears to coon-skin caps, and adding mirrors to make everything look bigger — and more enticing. It became the nation's largest independent oil company before it was sold in 1963.

The slogan, however, was never trademarked, so family members revived the Billups name and motto in 2018, opening a '50s-themed diner in Biloxi, Mississippi, called Fill-Up with Billups. The familiar outstretched hand symbol was resurrected, except now it was holding a coffee cup.

Woco Pep, which started out in Alabama selling kerosene, hopped aboard the gasoline bandwagon in 1916 and spread across the South, as well. Its gasoline — which was supplied by Pure — was colored red, blue, or green depending on the octane rating. It also had, according to early advertising "that odor of power."

Pure had its own motto: "Be sure with Pure." It created a big footprint across the South by also forging alliances with other early regional distributors. Colonial Oil of Norfolk sold Pure gasoline in 43 Virginia and North Carolina counties, while Seaboard Oil of Florida switched to Pure from Indian Oil, and had more than 320 stations distributing the product by 1931.

The Pure brand was sold to Union 76 in 1963, and the name was phased out, only to be revived, along with the distinctive "gear" symbol, in the 1990s by a cooperative selling gas in 10 states across the South, from Louisiana to Virginia.

As service stations consolidated, they built their brand identities even further and sought to retain customers by offering consistent, reliable service; clean restrooms; and incentives for repeat business, like discounts and giveaways. They issued paper "courtesy" charge cards that could be used at their stations. You couldn't carry over any balance: They had to be paid in full every month. But they added to the convenience of buying gas if you didn't have cash in your pocket. In 1939, Standard Oil of Indiana mailed 250,000 of these paper charge cards to its customers unsolicited.

Trading stamps, collectible coins, toys for kids, and dining sets were among the items given away to loyal customers. One popular item at Texas-based Texaco in the 1960s was a fire chief helmet.

Meanwhile, as more cars hit the road and more roads continued to be built — especially in the post-World War II boom — more gas stations continued to go up along the side of the road. Not all of them were conventional box-types, either. The art deco style that started in the late 1930s was reflected on the road, as well. And other stations were built in various shapes and sizes just to draw motorists' attention.

A few of them, like the airplane at the beginning of this chapter, can still be found.

Top: An art deco-inspired station has been restored on U.S. 220 in Roanoke, Va. *Author photos*

Above and left: Esso used this sturdy "castle" style station for a while. These examples survive in Pulaski, Tenn., above, and along U.S. 1 in South Carolina, where the building now houses a title and loan service.

Gulf Oil went all out with this station in Miami Beach, which employed a nautical theme and also included a hotel in 1939. *Marion Post Wolcott, Library of Congress*

HIGHWAYS OF THE SOUTH

Above: A Shell station in the shape of a clamshell survives in Winston-Salem, N.C. There were seven of them in the region at one point, but this is the only one left.

Left: This Conoco station on Route 66 in Shamrock, Texas, was impossible for passing motorists to miss.

Top: A billboard advertising Gulf's "No-Nox" gas in Columbus, Ga., in May 1941. *Jack Delano, Library of Congress*

Above: Wally's Service in Mt. Airy, N.C., with replica of Sheriff Andy Taylor's car from *The Andy Griffith Show* out front in 2020. *Author photo*

Above: Abandoned Union 76 station at 7-Mile Ford on U.S. 11 in western Virginia, February 2021. *Author photo*

Left: Gas station at State Highway 3 and U.S. 19 in Sumpter, Ga., date unknown. *Library of Congress*

Roadside Stops

A family stops to check out a map outside the Florida Welcome Center in 1954. *Florida State Archives*

Are We There Yet?

When you're traveling from one place to another, you might not get all the way there before you have to make a pit stop.

Or see something so fascinating you just have to pull over.

Or stock up on supplies.

Over the years, enterprising farmers and businessmen have set up shop by the highways to offer drivers a respite from the road — and sometimes, their kids' impatience to get there. To get somewhere. To get anywhere. From visitor centers to fruit stands; from general stores to souvenir shops, there are plenty of places to stop on the way to your destination.

Fruit stands were among the earliest roadside stops, and they're still around today, although some have evolved into something significantly more.

Above: A roadside fruit stand photographed in February 1939 in Robstown, Texas, had barrels of fruit front and center, but the owners also advertised Coca-Cola and Borden's ice cream and milk. *Lee Russell, Library of Congress*

Right: Johnson's Peaches on U.S. 220 in north of Rockingham, N.C., in February 2021. *Author photo*

The Berry Patch on U.S. 220 in Ellerbe, N.C., with its strawberry-shaped ice cream shop. *Author photos*

The Berry Patch in North Carolina is a fruit stand with a massive twist. It's attached to an ice cream shop that recalls the giant orange fruit stands in California and Florida — except it's red and shaped like a strawberry. Billed as the world's largest strawberry-shaped building, it weighs in at four tons and was serving up 19 flavors of ice cream, as of 2021. Inside the fruit stand is a selection of fruits and preserves, along with T-shirts, scented candles, and other gifts.

The fruit stand's name carries a double-meaning: It was founded in 1995 by Lee Berry, who started out selling strawberries from the back of his truck at the location. His wife suggested something was needed to catch the eye of drivers on what was known as "produce highway," where fruit stands were already commonplace. The huge strawberry was the solution: It's 24 feet tall and took more than five months to build.

Why strawberries? As of 2014, North Carolina was the fourth-largest strawberry-producing state in the nation.

A weathered sign points the way to an abandoned fruit stand near the North Carolina-South Carolina state line. *Author photos*

An old gas stop is signed as "William's Produce Etc." along State Route 57 in Little Rock, S.C., north of Dillon, in 2021. *Author photo*

From Gas to Convenience

Other roadside stops evolved from good old-fashioned gas stations, which went into decline starting around 1970. Until that time, the number of service stations had grown with the number of Americans — fueled especially by the postwar baby boom. Soon, the promise of a car in every garage became a different reality for many: two cars in every garage, and a trade-in every couple of years.

Those cars kept getting bigger, too, which meant gas mileage didn't change much from the 1920s through the 1960s. Car engines that were more powerful and heavier ate up just as much gas as the Model T and its cohorts had in the early days.

Even a bit more.

Americans' appetite for gas guzzlers only increased in the middle of the century, and fuel efficiency dropped as low as 11.9 miles to the gallon in 1973, the year the Arab oil embargo created long lines and short tempers nationwide. A few years before that, fuel consumption hit its peak, at more than 750 gallons for a passenger car and about 950 for the average SUV or pickup.

Around that time, in 1970, the number of gas stations nationwide stood at a whopping 216,000. But as fuel efficiency rose, the number of stations fell. Just 111,000 of them were still operating by 1990, and fuel efficiency a year later was up 70 percent (to nearly 17 mpg) from its low in '73. The oil embargo had another effect, too: It ushered in the era of widespread self-service.

Some stations still had garages attached, but service attendants no longer met customers at the pump. Instead, retailers offered drivers the option of saving a few pennies by pumping their own gas, and most chose to do just that. With gas prices going through the roof thanks to OPEC, they needed to any price break they could get.

Early on, many gas stations sold a few extras in addition to fuel. The Louisiana Billups station at left sold cigarettes, and a tobacco farmer opened a station in North Carolina, below that sold both Coke and Pepsi in 1940.
Library of Congress

Top: High Grove Grocery in on U.S. 31E in High Grove, Ky., has been in business since the 1940s. *Author photo*

Above: This general store had a post office inside and gas pumps out front in Bynum, N.C., in the fall of 1939. *Marion Post Wolcott, Library of Congress*

As time went on, fewer and fewer stations maintained full garages, and centers that specialized in tire sales or oil, lube, and tune-up services began to replace them. Instead of garages, more gas stations added convenience stores — or convenience stores added gas.

It wasn't a new concept. Harlan Sanders had served up chicken and other goodies at his Kentucky Shell station way back in the 1930s, and general stores often had a pair of pumps out front, even back then. But the casual pairing became more of a marriage in the late 20th century, and the trend only continued into the 21st. Arco added ampm convenience stores to compete with 7-Eleven, Circle K, and others, which also dispensed gas at many of their locations.

How did this play out in the South?

In 2019, Shell had the most transactions across eight Southern states, while BP led the way in South Carolina, and Sunoco in the Virginias. Pure Oil, "the official fuel of NASCAR,"

This sign on U.S. 220 in southern Virginia says Dodge's General Store was established in 1872. With headquarters in Tupelo, Miss., it has stores in nine Southern states that sell gas. But the chain is better known for its fried chicken. *Author photo*

operated across 10 Southern states from Virginia across to Louisiana, and Marathon was also a common sight in the Mid-Atlantic region.

Elsewhere, however, convenience stores ruled the day. Kentucky's biggest gasoline seller was Speedway, which had more than 3,900 stores nationwide. QuikTrip, which was founded in Oklahoma and had more than 800 locations, topped the list of gas-dispensers in Georgia and also had a significant presence in South Carolina.

But in the Palmetto State, Circle K ranked at the top. The chain was founded in 1951 by Fred Hervey, who served three terms mayor of El Paso. He bought a group of three Kay's Food Stores there and expanded into Phoenix six years later, by which point he had a "circle of Kay's."

The chain doubled in size in 1984 when it acquired a chain called Little General stores, expanding into six Southern states. It gained widespread exposure five years later from the hit comedy *Bill & Ted's Excellent Adventure*, in which Ted (Keanu Reeves) famously utters the line, "Strange things are afoot at the Circle K." By 2021, it had more than 15,000 locations worldwide, including many in the South.

Its biggest rival was 7-Eleven, another chain that got its start in Texas — Dallas, to be exact — back in 1927, as the Southland Ice Company. Ice was still sold in blocks back then, rather than in plastic bags, and founder Joe Thompson decided to kill two birds with one stone: He stocked up on things like milk, eggs, and bread, and kept them cold using his ice, selling them to customers who didn't want to go all the way to the grocery store. With 16 locations in Dallas, he could offer just that sort of convenience.

Southland's ice docks, were located a distance away from the building, so customers could just drive up, load in, and drive off again. The company soon applied the same principle to gasoline, which it started selling as well.

In 1928, an employee brought a souvenir totem pole back from a trip to Alaska and put it out in front of a store. The place soon became known as a Tote'm Store, since customers toted away what they bought there. The name stuck until 1946, when the store changed its name to reflect its new hours: 7 a.m. to 11 p.m. The company added customers after the end of Prohibition by adding liquor and beer sales, but it remained strictly a Dallas phenomenon until the early 1950s, when it expanded into Florida, Maryland, Virginia, and Pennsylvania.

Although it started out selling ice, however, 7-Eleven's signature ice product, the Slurpee, didn't originate there. It actually started out at a Dairy Queen in Kansas City owned by a man named Omar Knedlik, whose soda fountain kept breaking down. He put some of the bottles in the freezer to keep them cool, but he left them in a little too long and, when he opened them, he found they'd turned into a slushy mix — which his customers actually liked.

He built a machine to make them and started selling them to convenience stores. One of them, 7-Eleven, licensed it in 1965 and adopted the name Slurpee to make it their own.

The company added to the appeal in the '70s by packaging the drink in "baseball trading cups" depicting big league stars and similar promotional plastic tumblers tied to other popular figures.

7-Eleven went bankrupt in 1990, but was purchased by a Japanese company, which still owned it as of 2021. It has continued to expand, and, in 2019, announced it was buying Speedway's 3,900-store chain, in a $21 billion deal to create a 14,000-store network in the United States.

Casey's General Store, recently rebranded as just Casey's, is mainly in the Midwest and Plains states, but also has locations in Tennessee, Arkansas, Kentucky, and Oklahoma. It started out as a three-bay garage in Boone, Iowa, which Don Lamberti converted into a gas station and convenience store, naming it after his friend and gas supplier Kurvin C. Fish (or K.C./Casey).

By 2021, Casey's had more than 2,000 locations, focusing on towns with a population of 5,000 or fewer people.

Other chains, such as Wawa, targeted larger cities. The company, which had more than 900 locations, started out in Philadelphia. Sheetz and RaceTrac, meanwhile each had more than 500 locations, including a number of them in the South.

Many of these businesses opened in the late 1950s and early '60s, after the new interstate system was established, setting up shop at off-ramps, sometimes in clusters where there was nothing else around. Wawa, founded in 1964, is named for a Philadelphia neighborhood but operates in several mid-Atlantic states, as well as Florida. Sheetz also started in Pennsylvania, but has locations in six states, including the Virginias, North Carolina, and Maryland.

In some places, they've almost become like big-box convenience stores. One example is Buc-ee's in New Braunfels, Texas, between Houston and San Antonio. Part of a chain of around 40 locations in eastern Texas (with a few in Florida and Alabama). Buc-ee's apparently decided to live by the motto that "everything's bigger in Texas." The New Braunfels location holds the world record as the largest convenience store, with more than 66,000 feet of retail space. It has 1,000 parking spaces, 120 gas pumps, 83 restroom stalls, 80 soda dispensers, and 31 cash registers. Another Buc-ee's, west of Houston, set the record for the longest car wash with a 255-foot conveyor.

But the Buc-ee's "bigger is better" mantra isn't limited to convenience stores.

This Sheetz location in Ridgeway, Va., is advertised by this interesting billboard just up the road on U.S. 220. Contrary to what the sign says, all drivers do want to leave their car eventually. *Author photos*

Truck stops have broadened their horizons, too. Pilot, Love's, Petro, Flying J, and Travel Centers of America (TA for short, which opened as Truckstops of America in 1972) opened convenience stores. Pilot later bought Flying J, and TA acquired Petro, though both companies retained their original names, and it's not unheard-of to see a Pilot across the freeway from a Flying J.

These businesses expanded with time, opening expansive convenience stores to go with their shower facilities, and often including hot dogs, pizza, fried food, and sandwiches, or branded fast-food counters from the likes of Subway. Some even included sit-down casual dining under brands like Denney's and Iron Skillet.

At the other end of the spectrum, some gas stations downsized after the era of self-service began. In some places, it became common for a station to consist of nothing more than a canopy and a small drive-up kiosk, where an attendant would take payment and perhaps sell cigarettes or other small items.

Dollar General is a common sight on the highways and byways of the South. Often, locations are in small towns and on rural stretches of road not served by other stores. *Author photo*

Not all convenience stores sold gas, either.

Many were successors to the small corner grocers, five-and-dimes, and general stores that used to dot the landscape. So-called dollar stores became common, especially in the 21st century. Among them: Family Dollar, Dollar Tree, and the ubiquitous Dollar General, which seemed to be almost everywhere on highways and rural roads in the South by 2020.

Family Dollar started out in Charlotte, North Carolina, back in 1959, expanding from there into Virginia, South Carolina, and Georgia in the 1960s. In South Carolina, the founder opened Myrtle Beach's first discount store in 1962 and embarked on a radio ad blitz, buying up 50 spots a day for $1 each on the city's only radio station. When other stores complained, it didn't matter: The store manager at Family Dollar and the radio station's manager were brothers.

Family Dollar remained a regional operation through its early years, and had 100 stores across the Southeast by the end of its first decade. In 2015, it was sold to Dollar Tree, but retained its own identity and had 8,200 stores across the country in 2020.

The only larger chain of discount stores started out in the South, too.

Dollar General began as retailer J.L. Turner and Son in Kentucky back in 1939, and expanded to 35 stores there and in neighboring Tennessee before turning its focus to discount pricing. Turner's son, Cal, got the idea from "Dollar Days" promotions at department stores, so he decided to open a store that sold everything for a dollar, all the time. The result was the first Dollar General store, which opened in Springfield, Ky., in the summer of 1955.

By 2020, the chain had more than 16,000 locations.

Cracker Barrel

Cracker Barrel had a different strategy: Instead of locations along rural roads, it built along interstates.

Founded in 1969, the company took the traditional concept of the general store and supersized it — not the way discounters like Walmart did, by focusing on discount items, but in a way that made just about *everything* bigger.

In the old days, around the turn of the 20th century, general stores were community gathering places where farmers and their families would buy, sell, gossip, and hang out. Some had post offices; others had telephone exchanges; still others had a dentist's office. It was a good place to keep warm during the winter, since most such places had a pot-bellied stove in the middle of the shop. Folks would gather 'round to swap stories or maybe play checkers as they took the chill out of their bones.

You could get pretty much everything you needed there: a general selection of products that lent these stores their name. On the shelves, you'd find everything from tobacco to spices; from nuts and beans to candy. Fabrics, soap, dishes, and cooking utensils were also sold there; dried meat hung from the ceiling, and bags of flour could be found stacked up on the floor beside barrels containing stacks of various products.

Like crackers.

Hence, the name "Cracker Barrel."

A general store in Wagoner County, Okla., as seen in June 1939. Note the barrel on the floor at right.
Lee Russell, Library of Congress

HIGHWAYS OF THE SOUTH

Cracker Barrel Old Country Store in Troutville, north of Roanoke, Va., between U.S. 11 and Interstate 81. *Author photo*

Cracker Barrel Old Country Store had a variety of items for sale, too, but the emphasis was on souvenirs, games, toys, and decorations. The food was available in the other room: a sit-down restaurant serving traditional Southern fare like catfish and fried chicken. Instead of a pot-bellied stove, there was a fireplace (everything was bigger, remember). And out front, you could fill up your tank with Shell gasoline.

Founder Dan Evins actually started out as a gas station owner. He just thought he could draw more customers if he added a restaurant. So he borrowed $40,000 to do just that, opening the first Cracker Barrel off Interstate 75, on the outskirts of Lebanon, Tennessee. But even though he added the restaurant to boost gasoline sales, things didn't quite work out that way: The restaurant was a booming success, but the gas just wasn't flowing — especially when prices soared during the oil embargo. So Evins terminated his distribution contract with Shell in 1974, and by the end of the decade, none of his locations were selling gas.

The first Cracker Barrel was so successful that four more opened in as many years, in Manchester, and Caryville, Tennessee; Dalton, Georgia; and Franklin, Kentucky. By 1983, the company had 27 locations on interstates across seven Southern states.

Chewing the fat around the barrel at "The Country Grocery," an illustration by Otto Lange that appeared sometime between 1890 and 1910 in Judge, a satirical magazine published from 1881 to 1947. *Library of Congress*

Restaurant Hospitality attributed the chain's success to "its unrivaled ability to evoke nostalgia without being corny" and stores that are "old-fashioned, but are never cute." One reason for that is that the antiques inside are all real, not reproductions. The chain buys them for display, although there's no real chronological or geographical theme to them.

If there's a long line of people waiting to get in, customers have a way to relax while they wait in one of the many rocking chairs out front, similar to those you'll find on many porches throughout the region. If you like them, you can buy one.

As of 2020, Cracker Barrel had grown to more than 660 stores in 450 states. But when it tried to expand its business to supply grocery stores, it ran into legal trouble. It's natural to wonder whether Cracker Barrel makes a cheese product by that name that's available in grocery stores. The answer is no: It's made by Kraft. Still, it's a good question — and one that caused problems for the chain when it started placing products like bacon, turkey, and ham in supermarkets. Kraft noticed this took exception, because it been selling cheese under the Cracker Barrel name since more than a decade before the store/restaurant chain was founded. In the end, a settlement was reached in 2013 under which the chain continued to sell the products, but under a different name: CB Old Country Store.

Souvenirs Stands

Many convenience stores sell souvenirs like baseball caps, T-shirts, fridge magnets, and other items that say, "I was there." But selections are limited. Never fear, though, because a number of businesses have set up shop to offer a broader array of merchandise, from rugs, to pictures, to flags.

A painter's roadside souvenir stand in Corpus Christie, Texas, in February 1939.
Lee Russell, Library of Congress

Top: Souvenir stand between Washington and Baltimore in June 1940. **Above:** A stand selling pottery, vases, and birdbaths in Maryland, also in 1940. *Jack Delano, Library of Congress*

What's sold at roadside stands can run the gamut, as illustrated by these two photographs.

Top: A huge candy factory alongside Route 66 in Missouri in 2019.

Right: What looks like an old church converted into a store selling merchandise promoting Donald Trump's 2020 re-election campaign for president was still doing business on U.S. 220 in Boone's Mill, Va., after the votes were counted.
Author photos

A 1941 postcard shows souvenirs being sold along Peacock Alley in Georgia, a 30-mile stretch of U.S. 41 in the Dalton area where families would display bedspreads, quilts, rugs, and other crafts for sale, many of them bearing the image of a peacock.

Bang for Your Buck

Many places in the South, fireworks are sold year-round, and people from neighboring states often travel across state lines (from, say, North Carolina to South Carolina) to buy sparklers and Roman candles at permanent firework stands. Alabama, Arkansas, Georgia, Kentucky, and Mississippi all have relatively unrestricted laws on sales, too.

Some of those fireworks are illegal in nearby states, but that doesn't stop residents from trekking to South Carolina, in particular, to load up on them before Independence Day, or on any other occasion.

If you're driving into South Carolina from Georgia or North Carolina, you'll be bombarded with the sight of huge fireworks "stands" that are more like superstores.

Fireworks stores just south of the North Carolina-South Carolina state line offer a far bigger selection than your typical Fourth of July fireworks corner stand. *Author photos*

Fun and Games

You can (supposedly) see seven Southern states from this vista point on Lookout Mountain, Georgia *Author photo*

Delightful Diversions

Before Disneyland and Universal Studios hogged all the attention, a host of smaller attractions dotted the landscape, most of them situated right along the highway. Some were scary, some quirky, and others just plain fun, these amusement stops were a fixture of the American road trip. From roller skating to bowling to drive-in movies, from dinosaur parks the Wild West museums, you could find them all without driving too far.

Before the arrival of interstates, you could just pull off the road, hop out of the car, and treat the family to an afternoon of fun. These places were pit stops for some, destinations for others, ranging in size from the small traveling carnivals that still visit shopping center parking lots on occasion to acres of land filled with rides, games, and larger-than-life figures.

Bowling alleys, skating rinks, and drive-ins had their heyday in the 1950s, then began to decline in popularity as interstates made the roads where they were built obsolete. A few are still operating today, and the skeletons of others can be found sitting in overgrown fields and waiting to be torn down.

The number of operating drive-in theaters plummeted from a peak of 4,000 in the postwar malt shop era to barely 300. Bowling centers dropped from more than 12,000 in the mid-'60s to fewer than half that number by 2007. Roller rinks closed, and so did miniature golf courses, along with another mainstay: the sit-down movie theater. There are still plenty of those, but most of them used to be on highways at the center of the towns through which they passed. Those have long since given way to suburban multiplexes and locations in regional malls.

A bird's-eye view of Loew's Normandy Twin Open-Air Theatre, a Jacksonville, Fla., drive-in, seen in 1948. *Florida State Archives*

Above: The Gypsy Drive-In on Louisville Road (U.S. 31E) in 2021. Author photo

Left: The Gypsy in its heyday. *John W. Vomvoris, cinematreasures.com, Creative Commons 2.0*

Hiland Drive In on U.S. 11 in Rural Retreat, Va., opened in 1952 with a capacity of 200 cars. *Author photo*

Top: Hull's Drive-In on U.S. 11 near Lexington, Va., opened in 1950 with room for 300 cars. Closed in 1998, it was reopened by a group called Hull's Angels in 2001 as the nation's only nonprofit, community-owned drive-in. *Author photo*

Above: Chalk Hill Drive-In opened on 12.5 acres along U.S. 80 between Ft. Worth and Dallas in 1941. This photo is from a year later. It closed in 1973 and was torn down the following year. *Arthur Rothstein, Library of Congress*

Above: The Moonlite Theatre on U.S. 11 near Abingdon, Va., opened in 1954 and closed in 2013, reopening briefly in 2016. It was included on the National Register of Historic Places in 2007.

Above: What remained of the screen at the Bessemer City Drive-In in North Carolina in 2020. *Author photos*

Top: Skyvue Twin Drive-In in Winchester, Ky., opened in 1948 and closed in 2015.

Left: Another Skyview, spelled differently, sits on U.S. 11 in Virginia. It opened in 1949 and closed in 1988, being converted for use by an equipment company.

Bottom: Eden Drive-In in Eden, N.C., remains open as of 2021. It opened in 1949. *Author photos*

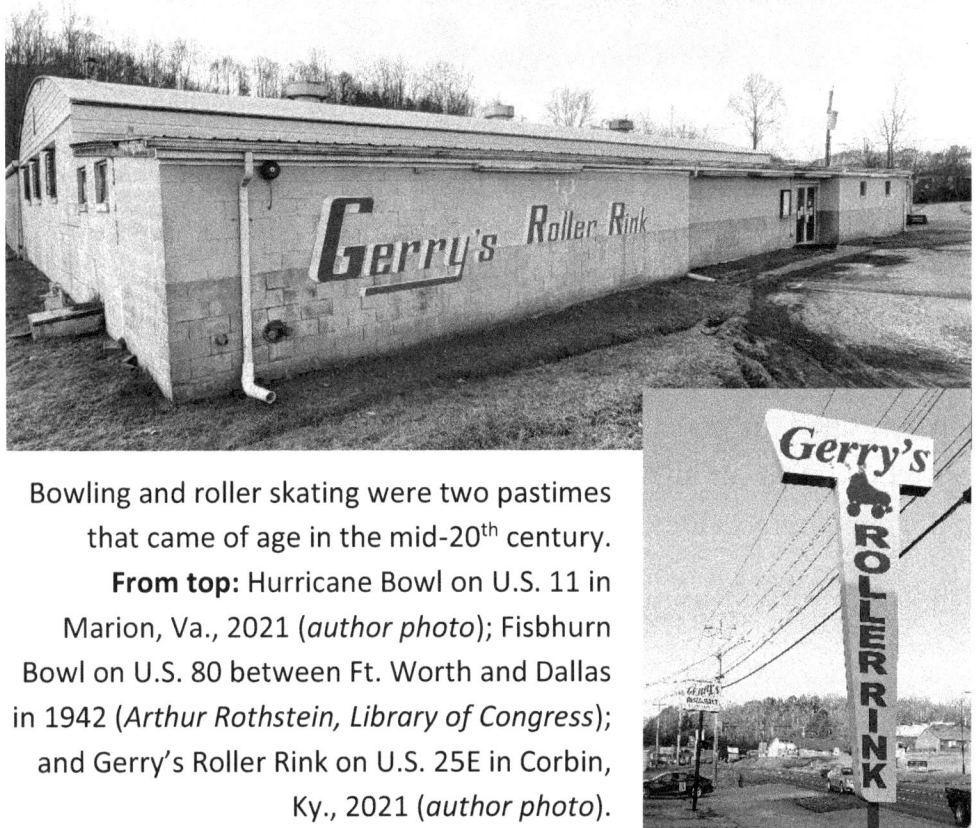

Bowling and roller skating were two pastimes that came of age in the mid-20th century. **From top:** Hurricane Bowl on U.S. 11 in Marion, Va., 2021 (*author photo*); Fisbhurn Bowl on U.S. 80 between Ft. Worth and Dallas in 1942 (*Arthur Rothstein, Library of Congress*); and Gerry's Roller Rink on U.S. 25E in Corbin, Ky., 2021 (*author photo*).

A polka-dotted elephant, one of numerous statues on the site, greets visitors to South of the Border in South Carolina, with giant mascot "Pedro" in the background. *Author photo*

Of course, there were larger attractions, too. South of the Border was a quirky roadside stop in South Carolina, just south of the North Carolina state line, that started out as a beer stand. Liquor was legal to sell there — unlike in the dry counties to the north, so people came across the border to buy it.

Alan Schafer called his pink cinder-block stand the South of the Border Beer Depot when he started the business in 1949, and he added a 10-seat grill a few years after that, offering hot dogs and burgers for sale after local politicians asked him to start selling food along with the beer to make it more respectable.

Business boomed, and Schafer soon discovered why.

"We found out that we were the only place on the highway between Fayetteville, N.C., and Florence, S.C., (a stretch of nearly 90 miles) that sold hot food," he said.

In 1954, he built a 20-room motel for those who wanted to stay the night at the halfway point between New York and Florida. It was a natural place for snowbirds to stop for the night on U.S. 301 when heading south or on the return trip north. And it was hard to miss the place. Schafer put up billboards along the highway pointing the way: some 200 of them on the roadside for 500 miles north and south of it.

South of the Border was a relatively modest establishment in the beginning, but "modest" isn't a word you'd use to describe it now.

A fireworks shop was added in 1964 for the same reason Schafer sold beer when he started out: Fireworks were illegal in North Carolina. Soon, South of the Border was a sprawling 300-acre tourist trap that included a post office, barbershop, campground, and saloon. As one writer put it, "If Las Vegas hooked up with Route 66 and had a baby, this would be it."

You can top off your tank at the gas station; grab a bite at the ice cream parlor, fast-food and sit-down restaurants; hold an event at the convention center; or buy a souvenir at one of half a dozen gift shops. There's also a reptile lagoon with 15 species of crocodilians and 50 kinds of snakes, as well as a "Pedroland" amusement park and a giant "sombrero tower." It isn't anywhere near Mexico, but Schafer played off the name he'd chosen for his business to create a geographical non-sequitur that wasn't exactly politically correct.

A bowlegged caricature of a Mexican bandit named Pedro that stands some 104 feet tall greets visitors as they drive in. Supposedly, it's the largest neon sign east of the Mississippi. It's also an example of the kind of ethnic stereotyping that sent the old Frito Bandito into retirement half a century ago, but Pedro survives, the largest among a plethora of statues that can be found on the site.

It was all based on a turn of phrase, one of Schafer's specialties. He invited visitors to "fill your trunk with Pedro's junque," and advertised "Yanqui prices, Pedro style."

They were cringe-worthy in more ways than one.

Ironically, though, Schafer — a man of Jewish heritage — was well known for his progressive views and practices. Black workers found employment at South of the Border in the still-segregated South, and Schafer also helped them register to vote. Customers of color were welcomed.

"If they had U.S. dollars, we took them in," he told the *Atlanta Constitution*. "It cost us some white customers at the time, but it was the right thing to do."

When Klansmen visited the place, he got his rifle and stood up to them, demanding that they get off his property.

Just a few of the sights at South of the Border in South Carolina.

Right: The giant sombrero tower, built in 1970 at a cost of $1.5 million, is visible from U.S. 301/501, as well as from the interstate.

Below: A giant Dachshund.

Bottom: A huge rabbit and an undersized brontosaurus in a sombrero look to hitch a ride outside "Ford Pedro." *Author photos*

HIGHWAYS OF THE SOUTH

Halfway across the country, on Route 66 in Missouri, lies another politically incorrect pit stop that's not quite as big as South of the Border, but it's headed in that direction. It's called Uranus, a planetary name that would have given Alan Schafer plenty of ideas for double-entendres.

"Uranus is expanding," signs on the property said in 2018. "Please excuse our mess."

Compared to South of the Border, Uranus is a babe by the roadside, bucking the trend against the kind kitschy attractions that have been dwindling in number for decades. You'll find a couple of them about an hour up the road in Stanton, where the Jesse James Wax Museum sits next door to the Antique Toy Museum and an abandoned gas station. "If You Were Ever A Kid, You'll Love The... TOY MUSEUM," a sign on the property enthuses, but the place is closed these days, and apparently has been for some time.

In 2007, though, you could pay $4 to check out a collection of 3,000 antique toys, most of which were either dolls and doll houses or transportation-themed toys on wheels.

As to the Jesse James Museum, it claimed to offer evidence that the outlaw wasn't killed in 1882 but actually survived and lived in Texas under an alias for 70 more years. Both attractions were doubtless built to waylay travelers on their way to nearby Meramec Caverns, a 4.6-mile underground network that became a tourist attraction during the Great Depression. But the two lonely buildings looked closed and/or deserted in 2019.

Uranus, though, has been thriving.

There wasn't anything there except a strip club (founded in 2000), until owner Louie Keen added a fudge factory in 2015 and applied the name Uranus. Suddenly, everything had a double meaning.

By 2020, Uranus included a tattoo studio, bar and grill, shooting range, escape rooms, and an axe-throwing attraction dubbed the Uranus Axehole. There was also a museum highlighting circus sideshow acts like a sword-swallower, along with such curiosities as a "unicorn skull" and a collection of two-headed animals. Uranus is also home to the world's largest belt buckle. Who might be able to wear it is anyone's guess.

The grounds are decorated with diverse objects like as a vintage police car, a rocket ship, and the old standby: dinosaurs. The strip club moved to Uranus, but Keen insisted that his unincorporated "town" (population: 25) is family friendly. "Family fun is in Uranus," one billboard proclaimed, and the candy shop is indeed a draw for the kids — most of whom have no idea that the "Fudge Packers Union" referred to on mugs in the gift shop has a secondary, less-than-wholesome meaning.

The Uranus police car, right, and the attention-grabbing road sign, which features a T-rex munching on a spaceship carrying the Flying Spaghetti Monster. *Author photos*

A double-decker bus emblazoned with a dinosaur chasing the Route 66 shield sits in "The Funk Yard" at Uranus. *Author photo*

There's also a newspaper called the Uranus Examiner, which claims it is "getting to the bottom of the big stories in Central Missouri."

Really.

If anyone complains about the name, employees just ask them what they've got against the planet.

Natural Wonders

From caves to mountains to natural rock formations, a number of attractions in the South are built on Mother Nature's foundation. And almost inevitably, opportunists set up kitschy businesses nearby to capitalize on the draw.

The pop-culture museums set up near Meramec Caverns on Route 66 are just one of many examples. The big attraction on U.S. 11, just south of Lexington, Virginia, is another.

It's a massive limestone arch that sits on land surveyed by George Washington in 1750, which later belonged to Thomas Jefferson. He bought it as part of a 157-acre purchase from King George III in 1774 for 20 shillings, an even bigger bargain than the Louisiana Purchase. He built a log cabin nearby, and hosted luminaries such as future presidents James Monroe and Martin Van Buren there.

Author Herman Melville mentioned it in *Moby Dick* as he described the appearance of the famed fictional whale as follows: "But soon the fore part of him slowly rose from the water; for an instant his whole marbleized body formed a high arch, like Virginia's Natural Bridge."

Natural Bridge around 1900. *Library of Congress*

Author William Cullen Bryant called Natural Bridge one of the continent's two most remarkable features, alongside Niagara Falls, in 1884. And Jefferson himself said it was "so beautiful an arch, so elevated, so light, and springing, as it were, up to heaven, (that) the rapture of the Spectator is really indiscribable [sic]!"

In 1927, lighting engineer Phinehas Stephens installed a series of colored lights that were used to illustrate an evening show called *The Drama of Creation.* President Calvin Coolidge pressed a button to start the first show, which was repeated every evening at sunset and continues today.

Just up the road on Highway 11, you can find other attractions that were built as diversions for travelers visiting the bridge. The Natural Bridge Zoo, which opened in 1972, sits on one side of the road, and Dinosaur Kingdom II — a fanciful attraction that depicts dinosaurs playing a role in the Civil War — is just across the street.

Natural Bridge Zoo offers elephant rides and includes such animals as a camel, giraffe, and various reptiles. *Author photo*

A Civil War soldier battles a dinosaur atop a train car at the entrance to Dinosaur Kingdom II near Natural Bridge, Va. *Author photo*

Perhaps an even more popular natural wonder was a series of caverns in Kentucky, the most prominent of which was Mammoth Cave, the largest network of caverns in the world. Indigenous peoples traveled its tunnels as far back as 4,000 years ago, and it wasn't long before European settlers started to exploit it.

Tours began in 1816, and a hotel was built.

Then, in 1839, a physician named John Croghan bought the cave for $10,000. He expanded the hotel and improved the roads, continuing the tours even as he set up a tuberculosis hospital in the cave. Fifteen patients were housed in stone cabins and wooden structures underground, where Croghan thought the climate would be good for them. It turned out not to be: The patients actually got worse, due in part to smoke from the oil lanterns used to light the cave. Five of them died, and the rest left within five short months, and Croghan himself ironically died of tuberculosis six years later.

But his improvements helped unleash a tourist-industry gold rush, and soon Mammoth Cave wasn't the only game in town. Diamond Caverns was discovered nearby in 1859, and the town of Horse Cave was founded around the same time. There's a cave there, but connection to any horse is unclear. According to one story, a farmer got drunk one night and drove his team of horses off a 50-foot-high bluff. One of them fell into the cave, and the town grew up around it.

The town briefly renamed itself Caverna — a name that survives on schools and in other places nearby — but was forced to change it back because the railroad objected.

The cave itself got a new name in 1916, when "Hidden River Cave" was chosen in a contest. When steps were added and it was opened to the public, it began to compete with Mammoth Cave for tourists. Soon enough, the *Louisville Courier-Journal* reported, it seemed that "every family in the neighborhood of Mammoth Cave for miles around" had "a separate family cave."

The reporter recounted stopping at a farmhouse to ask a boy for a drink of water several miles from Mammoth Cave.

"Have you ever been to Mammoth Cave?" he asked. "How far is it from here?"

"Mammoth Cave?" the boy replied. "What do you want to go there for? We've got a cave back out behind the barn that's got Mammoth Cave skinned by a mile."

By the 1920s, a host of caves like the Great Onyx Cave, Great Crystal Cave, Fern Cave, and others were competing for tourists. Cave salesmen set up tables beside the road and stopped cars as they approached. One even claimed to have discovered a "new entrance" to Mammoth Cave and was charging admission. Others were selling rocks, or chicken dinners at 75 cents a pop.

There was even a hotel built at the supposed "new entrance" called the New Entrance Hotel.

Naturally.

But the Mammoth Cave folks didn't take too kindly to this. In fact, they filed a lawsuit seeking $200,000 against the "new entrance" operator, the hotel owner, and a tour bus company. The bus operator was accused of promising tourists to drop them off at Mammoth Cave, only to deposit them at the so-called "new entrance" instead.

The "new entrance" guy would allegedly station agents on the public highway. There, they would harass representatives of the *real* Mammoth Cave and keep them from telling motorists where the legitimate entrance could be found. Meanwhile, he paid a fee to the bus company for every passenger diverted to the "new entrance" from the actual one.

Clockwise from top: Visitors to Mammoth Cave pose beside a stone structure built in the 1830s for tuberculosis patients, in this photo taken around 1912; the cave entrance; exploring by boat; stalactites in the cave. *Library of Congress and National Park Service*

A judge issued an injunction against the upstart company in 1926, but the operators of the real Mammoth Cave were still worried enough to take out a nearly half-page ad in the *Louisville Courier-Journal* on Sept. 5 headlined "CAUTION!" to warn potential customers against falling prey to any chicanery.

A national park was authorized for Mammoth Cave that same year, which was also the same year the federal highway system was set up. (The eastern and western branches of U.S. 31 are within a few miles of each other in Horse Cave.) As might be expected, motels and tourist cabins were built to accommodate visitors driving into both Horse Cave and nearby Cave City. The latter was founded around 1860 as a resort town for visitors to Mammoth Cave, and it still has a small population of just over 2,000. A large percentage of the people who sleep there are tourists, and vintage motels line U.S. 31W on the way into town from the north. The most distinctive is Wigwam Village No. 2, a row of tepee-shaped cabins built in 1937.

Owner Frank Redford actually built his first one in Horse Cave four years earlier, but it's no longer there. The owner would eventually develop five more Wigwam Villages: one each in Alabama, Arizona, California, Florida, and Louisiana. Of those, only the Arizona and California locations survive, both on Route 66.

Wigwam Village in Orlando, Fla., in 1951. *Florida State Archives*

Top: Wigwam Village No. 2 in 1940. *Marion, Library of Congress*
Above: The Cave City tepee cabins today. *Author photo*

HIGHWAYS OF THE SOUTH

In Cave City, wigwams are arrayed in a semicircle, in a variation on the motel court. They're not your typical canvas or animal skin tepees; they're much sturdier. One account described them as being made "by the novel process of blowing cement onto steel network frames." There was once a neon sign out front, along with gas pumps, and a circular lunch counter inside what Redford advertised as "The Largest Wigwam in the World," weighing in at 50 tons and rising 50 feet high.

Signs for the Star and Cave Land Motels on U.S. 31W in Cave City, 2021. *Author photos*

Cave City isn't right at the entrance to Mammoth Cave, though — it's about half an hour up the road. If you want to stay closer, you can check into a vintage cabin right across the parking lot from the park entrance.

The cabins date back to at least 1939, and plenty of visitors stayed there, as well as at the nearby hotel.

More than 80,000 people went through the cave in 1940, and 40,000 more visited the area. To make guests feel at home on their vacation, the hotel was getting ready to add an outdoor dining pavilion, two tennis courts, four shuffleboard courts, an auto-repair shop, and seven miles of new foot trails.

You could stay at the hotel all year, but the cabins were only open in the summer. In 1942, a night's stay would cost you $2 or $2.50, plus 50 cents more for each additional guest. "All cabins have hotels and showers," a pamphlet assured prospective guests.

Top: Vintage cabins at Mammoth Cave in 2021.
Above: A billboard on the road to Mammoth Cave. *Author photos*

Dinosaur World is one of the many attractions that sprang up in Cave City and on the road to Mammoth Cave. There's also a haunted house nearby, along with rock shops, canoeing, and an amusement stop featuring horseback, miniature golf, go-karts, and bumper cars. *Author photo*

Rock City

When you think of amusement parks, you might think of roller-coasters, merry-go-rounds, and Ferris wheels. But Walt Disney put a spin on the traditional park rides by giving them themes: You didn't just go fast, you got to see fanciful scenes during fantastic journeys on Pirates of the Caribbean or Small World.

But Disney wasn't the one who first imagined that concept. In 1947, Frieda and Garnet Carter commissioned Atlanta sculptor Jessie Sanders to carve out an underground tribute to nursery rhymes and fairytales atop Lookout Mountain. When it was complete, their Fairyland Caverns offered visitors a walking tour past dioramas depicting everything from Little Red Riding Hood to Cinderella. It was the same kind of magical journey you'd later take on Disney's themed rides — just on foot, and without the moving parts.

The Lover's Leap vista point on Lookout Mountain in Georgia. *Author photo*

At the end of the trail is Mother Goose Village, a giant display of fairytale scenes at the center of a large room that opened a decade later. The entire underground labyrinth is illumined by blacklight to create deep vivid hues that leave a lasting impression.

It was certainly an original idea, but the Carters had a lot of them.

They bought 700 acres atop of the mountain in 1924 with plans for a hotel and housing development. The streets were laid out and given fanciful names Robin Hood Trail, Peter Pan Road, Aladdin Road, and Gnome Trail. Gnomes were a favorite of Frieda Carter, who collected them in the form of German figurines; these she placed in a rock garden that became the mountain's first attraction. Of course, the mountain itself was a draw: From one spot called Lover's Leap, it's said that you can see seven states.

Whether that claim is true or not, the mountain is just a few miles from the place where Georgia, Alabama, and Tennessee converge. It's just a short drive from Chattanooga, and it offers a breathtaking view of the valley below. Folks had been going up there for decades by the time the Carters bought the place, and it was the site of a key Civil War battle, won by the Union.

It was already being called Rock City by then, because of its crevices, rocks, and other geological formations. But Garnet Carter marketed the heck out of it by painting the name on some 900 roadside barns that invited motorists to "See Rock City." (Some of them can still be found, and there are billboards along the highway, too.)

In addition to Frieda Carter's fairy rock garden, he came up with another idea to draw tourists: a tiny golf course. In keeping with his wife's fairytale theme, he dubbed it Tom Thumb golf — the nation's first miniature golf course — and patented the idea in 1927.

He opened the course on Lookout Mountain, and it was so popular that thousands of them were built in just the next few years. The original course is gone, except for the first hole, which has been preserved at Rock City.

Above: A sign on U.S. 11 in Alabama points the way to Rock City, 2021. *Author photo*
Inset: A man stands on Umbrella Rock at Lookout Mountain in 1928. *Library of Congress*

A pair of Rock City barn signs along U.S. 31E in Kentucky. *Author photos*

Food and Drink

The Chick 'N Pig Dining Room in Jacksonville, Fla., offered two Southern staples — pork and chicken — available in the dining room or via curb service in 1948. *Florida State Archives*

All the Fixin's

Southern cookin' is as diverse as the region itself. You'll find catfish in Mississippi, jambalaya and crawfish (or is it crayfish?) in Louisiana, and peaches in Georgia. Along the Atlantic Coast, you can feast on seafood, grits, and rice. In Appalachia, they serve up dishes of wild game.

Texas and Oklahoma like beef, while pork is popular elsewhere — even though fast-food pioneer Pig Stand got its start in the Lone Star State. Ham is big in Virginia, along with pulled pork and barbecue, aka BBQ. Chicken, especially fried chicken, is popular all over.

Biscuitville along U.S. Highway 29 in Danville, Va., closed its dining room during the COVID-19 pandemic in 2020. As of this printing, it had more than 60 locations, many along highways, in Virginia and North Carolina. *Author photo*

When it comes to side dishes, collard greens (a variety of cabbage), black-eyed peas, green beans, okra, and butter beans are common fare. Succotash, a mixture of lima beans, butter beans or pinto beans and sweet corn, often with other ingredients, is popular; so is coleslaw. Cornbread, hushpuppies, and buttermilk biscuits are staples: There's even a chain of restaurants called Biscuitville in Virginia and North Carolina.

Desserts is often a cobbler or chess pie: a simple recipe of eggs, butter, and sugar, along with either flour or corn meal and perhaps a thimbleful of vinegar. Flavoring can be used, too, or pecans (pecan pie is a variation on chess pie). The name has nothing to do with rooks or pawns; it's likely a variation on the word "cheese." Deep-fried pastries called fritters may be served, with beignets popular in New Orleans.

With such a variety of food being prepared across the region, it's no surprise that enterprising Southerners wasted little time opening up restaurants, coffee shops and diners to serve the motoring public.

HIGHWAYS OF THE SOUTH

Diners remain popular in the South. **From top:** Little Chef on Main Street and Tammy's on U.S. 58 in Danville, Va.; Shell's Bar-B-Q on Springs Road in Hickory Springs, N.C. *Author photos*

Diners started out as restaurants on wheels, first in wagons and later in converted rail cars. The latter are still sometimes used or emulated. Their close cousins are coffee shops, "greasy spoons," and drive-ins, which can still be found along Southern roads, though they're less common than they were in the era before big chains and fast-food outlets.

A truck driver and a sailor at the counter in a Louisiana coffee shop on U.S. 90 in 1943. *John Vachon, Library of Congress*

There's a huge difference between your classic coffee shop and the chain coffeehouses of today like Starbuck's. Sure, they both serve coffee, but the similarities end there.

Modern coffeehouses serve $5 "designer" drinks like lattes and ice-blended drinks with caramel, chocolate chips, and a variety of other non-coffee ingredients. It's like a coffee shop and an ice-cream parlor had a baby. A large portion of their customers are students and young professionals on the go, many of whom bring along their laptops and earbuds for company. They're built more for the city than the highway, although you can find them there, too, most often at open-air retail centers beside interstate off-ramps.

Coffee shops serve coffee, too, but without the frills. During their heyday in the 1940s and '50s, they set up shop along old highways before there were off-ramps and catered to weary truckers and travelers who used coffee as an antidote for droopy eyelids rather than a flavor-filled treat. Back when they got started, a cup o' joe was 5 cents, not 5 bucks, with optional cream and sugar. Laptops wouldn't be invented for decades, but you might read a newspaper in a leather booth or on a swivel stool at the counter.

Breakfasts were big (because you usually had coffee for breakfast), both in terms of helping size and popularity, but the menus also included things like cold turkey and chicken salad sandwiches, meatloaf, and chicken-fried steak. Waffles were frequently a signature breakfast item, but some places that served them were just as well known for their steaks. And steak houses like Clarence's on U.S. 220 in Ridgeway, Virginia, drew a breakfast crowd, too.

The Hub, a diner/coffee shop up the road at the intersection of State Route 40 and old U.S. 220 in Rocky Mount dates back to 1935. Decades later, you could order oatmeal, biscuits and gravy, or pork chops and eggs for breakfast; or stop by for a dinner of liver and onions, country ham, or crab cakes.

Clarence's in Ridgeway, above, and The Hub in Rocky Mount, in 2021. *Author photos*

As time passed, some standalone coffee shops expanded into chains, many of which were prominent in the South.

The Waffle House got the waffles-and-steak formula down to a science, becoming the McDonald's of coffee shops with more than 2,000 locations in 25 states as of 2021. (In fact, by 2005, there were 10 Waffle Houses and just nine McDonald's in Macon, Georgia.) It wasn't the first eatery to use "Waffle House" in its name: There was a Waffle House in Pennsylvania way back in 1884. A visitor was so impressed that he reported: "The best waffles, steaming hot, and one at a time were served, by one of the smartest old ladies he had ever met."

K.C. Waffle House in Drumright, Oklahoma, was operating in the early years of the 20th century, and so was a Two Girls Waffle House up in Anchorage, Alaska. A Waffle House in Kennewick, Washington, beckoned customers with a sign that bragged about its "Good EATS!"

The modern Waffle House, however, didn't get its start until 1955 in the Atlanta suburb of Avondale Estates. Real estate agent Tom Forkner teamed up with Joe Rogers, who was working as a regional manager for a chain of roadside diners called Toddle House. It wasn't exactly a leap of faith for Rogers, who stayed with his former employer for six years even as he embarked on his new venture. It made sense because the Toddle House chain was thriving. It had hundreds of locations, all with the same simple layout: a row of stools at a stainless-steel counter inside a small brick cottage with a blue gabled roof.

The chain, however, was purchased by a competitor in the 1960s and eventually went out of business.

Waffle House was another story, though it followed a similar format.

The owners gambled that they could attract more customers by being open 24 hours at a time when only one other restaurant in the city operated around the clock. There were 16 items on the menu, and the business sold more waffles than anything else, which is how they came up with the name. The sign was painted yellow to attract passing motorists to the restaurant, which was designed to capitalize on the postwar boom in highway travel.

A second location opened in 1959, and the chain had 48 restaurants by the end of the 1960s. By 2019, it had locations in half the 50 states, the vast majority of them in the South. Its home base of Georgia led the way with nearly 440 locations, with Alabama, both Carolinas, Tennessee, and Texas were each home to well over 100.

Left: Waffle House restaurant in Mt. Airy, N.C., 2020. *Author photos, left and center*

Waffle House interiors follow a fairly standard blueprint that includes some booths and a counter. Compare the photo from 2021, above, with the scene captured in a 1959 newspaper ad, at right.

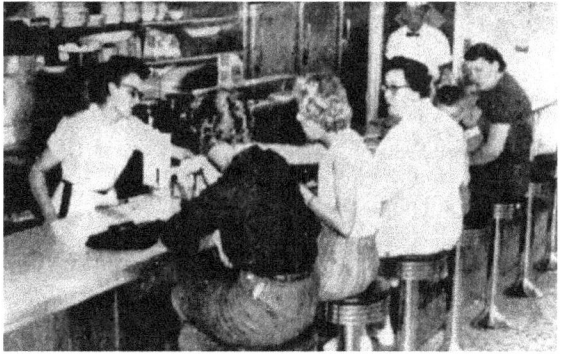

Above: Waffle House's signature menu item is overlaid on a photo of the first Waffle House location as it appeared in 2021. *Author photo*

Right: The same location in a postcard. Notice the sign has been changed slightly, though it retains the lettering style and arrow. *Author collection*

Waffle House's 24-hour schedule was so reliable that the federal government adopted a "Waffle House Index" to establish how much assistance might be required after a hurricane or tornado. If the index was green, it meant the Waffle House was serving a full menu; yellow indicated a limited menu, because the restaurant had no power, was short on food, or was on a generator; red meant the restaurant was closed.

The original Dwarf House in Hapeville, Ga., is still open, though it bears the Chick-fil-A branding prominently. A statue of founder Truett Cathey sits on the bench out front. *Author photo*

Chicken and More Chicken

Oddly enough, Waffle House once signed an agreement to sell an innovative menu item from another soon-to-be famous Atlanta-based eatery: a fried chicken breast nestled between two buns known as the Chick-fil-A. But the menu item reportedly got so popular that it outsold offerings, so Waffle House backed out.

The Chick-fil-A chain started out in 1946 as a restaurant called the Dwarf Grill, which was indeed small: It had just four tables and 10 counter stools, along with a jukebox. Like Waffle House, the restaurant in the Atlanta suburb of Hapeville, Georgia, was open 24 hours a day... except on Sundays (when Chick-fil-A remains closed to this day). Founder

Truett Cathy said he adopted the policy "because it gives our employees a chance to rest and start off a new day. And I can't think of anything more distasteful than facing a sinkful of dirty dishes in the middle of a Sunday Afternoon."

Hamburgers were the biggest seller at the Dwarf Grill, at 20 cents, and the Dwarf House also served peach pies and Cokes for a nickel each. The priciest item was a 7-ounce ribeye with fries and rolls, at 90 cents.

Cathy eventually tweaked the name to Dwarf House and tied his concept to Snow White and the Seven Dwarfs. The original location had a miniature door out front and motorized display in the back, which featured the dwarfs attached to a chain that moved them from the cottage on one side of a mural to the mine entrance on the other.

A second eatery, on State Highway 54 in nearby Forest Park, got a mural of the fairy-tale characters, too; that restaurant was destroyed in a 1960 fire that caused an estimated $75,000 in damage.

Cathy had surgery around the same time, and it appeared the Dwarf House chain would get no bigger. When he sought to rebuild the Forest Park eatery, he decided to open a self-service window, but knew right away that he'd made a mistake ("I had as many problems as I really wanted") and decided to lease it out — ironically enough to Kentucky Fried Chicken — and focus on his Hapeville restaurant.

He'd already begun tinkering with the idea of a chicken steak sandwich. That was his original name for it, but it ended up being called a Chick-fil-A. He opened up a small "hole in the wall" shop at the Greenbrier Shopping Center in 1962 to showcase the new sandwich, which he sold for 50 cents and touted as "the first new fast-food item in the last 50 years."

"They're still trying to do something different to a hamburger," he told the *Atlanta Constitution* in 1979. "Make them teeny-weeny, double-decker, but it's still a hamburger. Hot dogs are the same way. Eight-inch dog, foot-long dog or a 36-inch dog; still it's a hot dog."

The sandwich sold so well it became the foundation for a new chain with the Chick-fil-A name that far outstripped the success of the Dwarf House — although about a dozen restaurants under the original name were still operating in 2020.

The number of Chick-fil-A sites, meanwhile, was closing in on 3,000.

In 1995, Chick-fil-A adopted an ad campaign featuring cows asking customers to "Eat mor chickin," a phrase that probably wasn't used at the Dwarf House, which still (gasp) served beef, too.

Although Chick-Fil-A rivals it in terms of popularity, many people still think of a different chain when it comes to fried chicken: KFC. Those initials originally stood for Kentucky Fried Chicken, and it was founded by Harland Sanders, an entrepreneur who was actually born in Indiana, not Kentucky. He was never a military colonel, either: He received the honorary title in 1935, the year he founded his first restaurant.

Before getting into the into the restaurant business, he'd made a tidy sum operating a ferry on the Ohio River. But he went bust after he invested his earnings in a company that made acetylene lamps, which were used by farmers who didn't have electricity. It seemed like a good idea... until Delco started producing electric farm lights. "Little by little, I lost everything I'd put into the business and would up broke," Sanders would write.

It wasn't the first job he'd had — or the first one he'd lost, for that matter. He'd worked as a railroad fireman and a lawyer, among other jobs. But he lost both positions after getting into fights: first on the railroad with a coworker, and as a lawyer with one of his clients. Yes, he had a temper, and those brawls weren't even the worst of it.

Later on, after he opened a Shell gas station on U.S. Route 25E in Corbin, Ky., he painted a sign that showed motorists how to get there. A competitor named Matt Stewart wasn't too happy about that, so he painted over the sign. When Sanders found out, the story goes, he threatened to blow Stewart's "goddamn head off" before repainting the sign.

Stewart, however, wasn't scared. He just painted over the sign again.

But Sanders caught him in the act, and ran after him along with a couple of armed Shell representatives. A gunfight ensued: The Shell manager was fatally shot, and Sanders pulled the gun from his hand and fired back, winging Stewart in the shoulder. Stewart was later arrested.

Sanders had gotten into the service station business by chance. After losing his shirt on the acetylene lighting venture, he'd gotten a job selling tires for Michelin. He bought a house that he could only reach via a swinging bridge, which was "built just for wagons, but I drove automobiles across it," Sanders recalled.

Big mistake.

"One frosty morning, I was pulling my son Harland Junior's car with my car to get it started," he later remembered. "Just when we were on the middle of that bridge, the right-hand cable broke and both cars flipped."

Sanders and his son both fell, and although his son came away with "only a little scratch," the not-yet-colonel was knocked out cold. When he came to, he found he'd broken his arm, and blood was gushing from between his fingers. "There wasn't a place on my body that wasn't black and blue, and my head was split from one of my eyebrows through my forehead."

He refused to see a doctor and tended to the wounds himself, then went back to work for Michelin, traveling around by bus to make sales. But without a car, it was an uphill battle, and the company let him go.

He hitchhiked to Louisville in search of work, but had no luck, so he started back again and got a ride from a gentleman who turned out to be the state manager for Standard Oil, and he wound up with a job pumping gas, checking tires, changing the radiator water... whatever his customers wanted. He developed a knack for it and a reputation for service, so a few years later, after leaving the Standard station, he opened a station for Shell in Corbin.

Shell had gotten wind of his success and offered him a sweet deal: He could have the service station rent-free if he gave the company a percentage of the sales.

When his customers started asking where they could find something to eat, he did what he'd always done.

He gave them what they asked for.

Sanders opened a small café, where he cooked up chicken, steaks, and ham, along with side dishes like spinach and collard greens. He had just six tables, but he advertised far and wide, painting signs himself on barns for 150 miles in every direction that touted "Sanders' Servistation and Café." (He called it a café because he could make the letters larger that way, instead of writing "restaurant.")

Business was so good he expanded from six tables to a full 142-seat restaurant in 1937, and on top of that, he added a motor court. The Sanders Court & Cafe offered tile baths with an "abundance of hot water," carpeted floors, "perfect Sleeper" beds, air conditioning, steam heating, a radio in every room. And, of course it was "serving excellent food."

But no fried chicken; at least not at first: "In those days, fried chicken took a long time to prepare. I didn't have the fast method that I worked up later," Sanders explained. "If I fried chicken and the customer didn't want fried chicken, it was wasted and you couldn't retrieve it."

The Sanders Café still exists in Corbin, Ky., on U.S. Highway 25E, the original site of Harland Sanders' first restaurant and service station. They don't sell gas there anymore, and the motor court is gone, but they still sell chicken. *Author photos*

The Robert E. Lee Motel in western Virginia on U.S. 11 had a Colonel Sanders restaurant upstairs in the 1940s and early '50s. The motel was torn down in 2009, but the sign was preserved and restored at a storage business nearby. *Author photo*

More expansion, and other locations, followed.

Sanders opened a second site in Asheville, N.C., also on Route 25E, in 1939. Then he added a restaurant on the upper floor of the Robert E. Lee Motel on the Lee Highway (naturally), U.S. 11, in Bristol, Virginia, during the 1940s.

A photo of Sanders graced the menu, together with the pledge, "I promise you a good meal. If it's not, don't pay for it." You could get a "generous portion" of Kentucky Fried Chicken, served "with all the natural goodness sealed in," for $2, and you could even get an extra plate if you wanted to share your portion with a youngster. Other items on the menu included fillet of catfish for $1.75, U.S. prime steak for $3.75, and pot roast beef for $1.95.

A family of six could stay at the motel for just $11 in the 1960s.

Sanders got out of the motel and sit-down restaurant business in 1955 in favor of selling franchises that became the basis for KFC.

The original café in Corbin has been renovated, and includes a museum, while the Asheville site has been converted to apartments. Kentucky Fried Chicken pulled out of the Lee Motel around 1954, and it closed in 1996, becoming a haven for homeless before it was demolished in 2009. The sign survives, outside a nearby storage business on U.S. 11.

This giant chicken in Marietta, Ga., was built in 1956 to take advantage of traffic on a newly built segment of U.S. 41, the first divided highway in Cobb County and a gateway to Atlanta, just to the south. The 56-foot-high hen didn't originally cluck for KFC; it was built for a restaurant called Johnny Reb's Chick, Chuck'N Shake, which was sold in 1966 and franchised to Kentucky Fried Chicken. *Author photo*

Kentucky Fried Chicken, 1903

Recipes for "Kentucky Fried Chicken" predated Harland Sanders' enterprise by at least half a century, as illustrated by this one, which was published under the simple headline "What to Eat." in the Harrisburg Star-Independent in May of 1903.

"Have a chicken killed the day previous to (prepare for) cooking. Split open at the back as for broiling. When ready to cook wipe dry and brush well with butter. Season with salt and pepper. Put into a pan with a slice or two of bacon and one cup of water. Set in the oven and baste frequently. When tender and nicely browned place on a hot dish with rice and serve."

The chain became known for its catch phrase "finger-lickin' good," which dates to 1956 and is said to have originated with Arizona franchisee Dave Harman, who was seen licking his fingers in the background of a TV commercial as he ate some of the Colonel's chicken. A viewer complained, and, according to legend, Harbaugh responded with the famous phrase.

But it may not be that simple. The slogan actually first appeared in newspaper advertising (as far as I could determine) three years earlier, in association with another restaurant entirely: Electric Lunch of Corvallis, Oregon, which also served baked ham, meatloaf, "smothered steak" and "fillet of red snapper."

In 1957, a rival product called Broasted Chicken was using it, too, along with another slogan proclaiming it the "world's finest eatin' chicken."

The following year, "It's finger-lickin' good" appeared in an ad for Kentucky Fried Chicken in the *Munster Times* of Indiana, but continued to be used by other companies, too — and not just for chicken, but for menu items ranging from spareribs to cod. Broasted Chicken was still using the phrase in its ads until at least late 1963. Eventually, however, it became firmly tied to KFC, which kept using it until the coronavirus pandemic of 2020 made it less appealing to lick your fingers. Its replacement, however, was the much less memorable: "So Good!"

Still, fingers aren't just for lickin' when it comes to chicken, and the Chick-fil-A sandwich wasn't the only innovation when it came to poultry fare in the South.

The exact origins of chicken fingers (aka chicken strips or chicken tenders) are somewhat hazy. Guthrie's, a family-owned restaurant in Alabama, opened its first location in 1965 and added an item called chicken fingers to the menu in '78. But Spanky's in Savannah, Georgia, seems to have stumbled onto the idea a couple of years earlier, when co-owner Alben Yarborough was trying to make a chicken breast sandwich and it wound up too big for the bun. So, he trimmed the edges and saved them, added some seasoning, fried them up and created the chicken strip.

Or did he?

Even before that, in 1970, a story buried on Page 8 of the *Montgomery Advertiser* in Alabama mentioned the eighth annual Alabama Products Luncheon, "consisting entirely of Alabama-grown or Alabama-processed foods." The menu included a host of familiar items, the last of which was "chicken 'fingers'."

Nowadays, they're sold pretty much everywhere, from fast-food restaurants to convenience stores. Zaxby's, which started in Athens, Georgia, opened in 1990 and made a name with its chicken fingers and variety of dipping sauces. As of 2020, it had locations in 14 states from Virginia down to Texas, as well as in Indiana, Kansas, and Utah.

George Church opened his first chicken stand across from the Alamo in San Antonio, Texas, in 1952. Long lines began to form: You could get two pieces of fried chicken and a roll for 49 cents. Expansion was gradual at first, with the business growing to 17 restaurants in five Texas cities by 1968. The philosophy was simple: Target the poor urban neighborhoods Kentucky Fried Chicken had been ignoring. The business incorporated the next year, and had more than 100 restaurants by the end of the decade.

Another popular chicken outlet in the South was founded in 1971 as Chicken on the Run, a place "so fast you get your chicken before you get your change." Owner Al Copeland started it in New Orleans after being inspired by Kentucky Fried Chicken. His chicken stand didn't make it, but Copeland was undeterred. He added some cayenne pepper and other Cajun spices to his recipe and tried again under the name Popeyes Mighty Good Golden Chicken — claiming he was too poor to afford the apostrophe for "Popeye's."

Business boomed, and a chain was born.

Although it had a license to use the cartoon character Popeye in its marketing for many years, Copeland said the name was inspired by Popeye Doyle, the detective played by Gene Hackman in 1971's hit film, *The French Connection*. Copeland bought Church's in 1989, but it proved an overreach, and he had to declare bankruptcy. The two chains eventually went their separate ways, with both finding success.

Popeyes had more than 3,000 locations as of 2020, while Church's had more than 1,000.

While Popeyes was named for a movie character, over in Charlotte, North Carolina, Bojangles — founded in 1977 — got its name from a popular tune from the same era, "Mr. Bojangles." The first franchise opened the following year, and by 2021, the chain had grown to more than 750 locations in 14 states, most of them in the South Atlantic states of North and South Carolina, Georgia, and Virginia. Like Popeyes, it also served a popular Southern dish: dirty rice, a dish flavored with meat and ingredients like onions, peppers, garlic and other spices.

Making a Stand for Pigs

As popular as chicken is across the South, it isn't the only game in town. Pork is a popular dish, as well, especially, barbecued or "pulled" pork.

The word "barbecue" come from "barbacoa," a term from the West Indes that means "to slow-cook over hot coals." In the antebellum South, plantation owners threw big festivals and church picnics where they got the best cuts and left the tough portions for the slaves. Not to be shortchanged, these slaves learned how to make those cuts just as tender by slow-cook barbecuing the meat over hot coals. They would "pull the pork" off the coals when it was done.

After the war, the practice continued. An 1876 announcement in the *Columbia Missouri Herald* declared: "There will be a Barbecue, with Music and Dancing, at the Old Barbecue Stand near the McBaine Bridge over the Perche, three-fourths of a mile south of Providence Church, and four and a half miles northwest of Columbia on Saturday, Sept. 16. The candidates for the various offices will be on the grounds and will address the people. The best of accommodations are offered at reasonable rates."

In the segregated South, Black Americans would barbecue meat in homemade cookers and sell it on street corners to their neighbors, because they didn't have the money to set up a permanent shop. Still, these makeshift barbecue stands proved so popular that white residents would secretly head out to pick some up.

Eventually, some of these neighborhood chefs scraped together enough money to open up roadside stands, sometimes with a few stools and tables, in a "barbecue belt" across the Deep South that stretched from Louisiana eastward to the Carolinas. In Kentucky, the barbecue process is applied to lamb, while in Texas, it's used on beef.

A Pig Stand in Dallas. *Author collection*

That's why it might come as a surprise to learn that the pork sandwich, not the hamburger, was the featured item on the menu at the Lone Star state's — and the nation's — first drive-in restaurant: Kirby's Pig Stand. There were carhops who delivered your meal to your car, and the Pig Stands were open 24 hours. The business even installed a neon light shaped like a grazing pig in the dining area of its San Antonio location all the way back in 1924.

But "Pig Stand?"

The name might not sound too appealing, but the concept was a huge hit when Jesse Kirby opened the first stand in Dallas at Chalk Hill Road and the Dallas-Fort Worth Turnpike (later U.S. 180 and, after that, State Highway 180).

The year was 1921, and like the improved highway, it was an idea whose time had come. Just three years later, there were 10 Pig Stands in Dallas, and the burgeoning chain had expanded into six other states, as well. The chain was among the first to start franchising, in 1925, and later pioneered such culinary favorites as chicken-fried steak, Texas toast and onion rings.

The signature item, though, was a Tennessee-style barbecued meal called the Pig Sandwich. By 1934, it was being sold at more than 120 locations. The core territory was Texas, Louisiana, Arkansas, and Oklahoma, but there were stands in Mississippi, Florida, and as far away as New York and California.

Leroy Vandegrift started one of them, Van's Pig Stand, in Shawnee, Oklahoma, back in 1930, where he sold Pig Sandwiches for 15 cents a pop. He added locations in Wichita, Kansas, and Wichita Falls, Texas over the years, and expanded the original site to include a basement charcoal steak house that operated for three decades. Van's was still going strong into the 21st century — after the rest of the chain had gone (pork)-belly up.

Frith's Dixie Pig has been in business since 1954 on U.S. 220 (now the business route) in Martinsville, Va. *Author photo*

The company's heyday came and went, and the chain contracted to just 23 locations, all in Texas, by 1961. The last Dallas restaurant closed in 1983, and the two remaining Pig Stands shut their doors in 2006, but a former carhop named Mary Ann Hill reopened the one in San Antonio that dates all the way back to 1927. And the Kirby's name lived on in the Kirby's Steakhouse chain founded in 1954 by Jesse's son, B.J. Kirby.

But Pig Stand wasn't the only barbecue eatery in the South. Not by a long shot. In 1939, Joe Bessinger opened South Carolina's Piggie Park Drive-In. A similar stand, Frith's Dixie Pig, opened in 1954 in Martinsville, Virginia. Both were still operating as of 2021, with the sign for Maurice's Piggie Park (named for Bessinger's son) towering over the Charleston Highway in West Columbia, one of nine locations in the area.

Right: The huge sign at Maurice's Piggie Park on the Charleston Highway in West Columbia looks like it would be right at home on the Las Vegas Strip.

Below: The drive-in "pit stop" area at Piggie Park outside the restaurant, which can be seen in the background. *Author photos*

Top: Big Chief Barbecue, Columbus, Ga., in December 1940. **Above:** Corrugated metal barbecue stand in Corpus Christie, Texas, February 1939. *Library of Congress*

Above: This sign rises high above the Smokey Pig on Louisville Road in Bowling Green, Ky.

Right: Bridges Barbecue Lodge in Shelby, N.C., opened in the late 1940s and moved to its present site on U.S. Highway 74 (Dixon Boulevard) in 1953. *Author photos*

Drive-Ins and Drive-Thrus

Pig Stand and Piggie Park were among the restaurants that catered to the burgeoning car culture of the mid-20th century by providing customers a new way to eat: In their cars. They didn't need to go into the restaurant. They could drive *in* and eat from a tray placed beside their rolled-down windows, or they could drive *through*, grabbing a bagged-up meal and taking it home to enjoy (if it didn't get cold along the way).

Pig Stand was a pioneer in both modes of service. In 1921, it began using carhops and side trays. Then, 10 years later, a franchise outlet in Los Angeles (Pig Stand 21) started giving customers bagged meals from a window in the building. The drive-through window — or "drive-thru," if you prefer — was born.

Drive-ins became a part of popular culture in the 1950s, as teens began congregating in their parking lots to hang out and listen to newly popular rock 'n' roll radio, but the popularity of drive-throughs was more enduring... and continued to grow. As of 2020, drive-through sales accounted for 70 percent of fast-food revenue.

Drive-ins are still around, too, sometimes combined with diners.

The Parkette in Lexington, Kentucky, still grabs motorists' attention today with its massive 40-foot sign on New Circle Road, a "ring road" around the state's second-largest city. There's a woman at the top carrying a drive-in tray, leaning forward as though she's about to do a swan dive. It cost $10,000 back in the day.

The sign wasn't there yet when the drive-in opened in 1952; it went up a couple of years later when the restaurant was still so far outside town that founder Joe Smiley said people laughed at him. "They said, 'You won't sell a dozen hamburgers a week out there."

At first, the street out front wasn't even paved. When it rained on opening night, the road turned into a muddy soup, and Smiley worried cars might get stuck and block the entrance. So he hired a tow truck for $35 to keep the roadway clear, and more than recouped his investment: Customers braved the storm to check out his new business, and he made $400 that first night.

There wasn't any indoor seating back then; the diner area was added later. All the carhops were females, like the "diving woman" on the sign. They wore wool uniforms like hotel bellhops and sat on bleachers, waiting to serve customers when they drove up. (Today, the place has intercoms to take orders.)

The Parkette's signature item was a double-deck cheeseburger with the works called the Poor Boy, which you could get with "enough fries to feed the family" for 45 cents. Those fries weren't frozen, either: They were brought in from Idaho by the train carload. The restaurant sold an estimated 19.2 million Poor Boys during its first 40 years in business. But there were other items on the menu, too: That giant sign advertises chicken, shrimp, and fish boxes, and today's fare includes burgers named with a nod to car culture, like the T-Bird, the Spare Tire, and the Backfire Burger.

Then there's "Our Famous Fried Chicken" — which originally went by another name. According to the *Lexington Herald-Leader*, Smiley sold that name to another fast-food entrepreneur for $30,000. That's how much Colonel Harlan Sanders paid him for the rights to "Kentucky Fried Chicken."

The Parkette sign in Lexington, Ky., 2021. *Author photo*

Top: A wavy awning awaits drive-in customers at the Sugar -n- Spice in Spartanburg, S.C. *Author photo*

Middle: Faivers in Tallahassee, Fla., c. 1950. *Florida State Archives*

Below: Dairy Center in Mt. Airy, N.C., 2020. *Author photo*

HIGHWAYS OF THE SOUTH

Dick's Drive-In in Leaksville (Eden), N.C., has been "the place to be since '63," according to a sign in its parking lot. Hot dogs are the signature item, but there's a full menu with more than 80 items from a pimento cheese sandwich to a flounder plate.
Author photos

Above and right: You'll find the Brown Cow Drive-In on U.S. Highway 25E, just south of Corbin, Ky.
Author photos

Left: "That Famous Falls City hi-Bru BEER" was on sale at The Big Orange, Amelia and Florida avenues in Tampa, c. 1946.
Florida State Archives

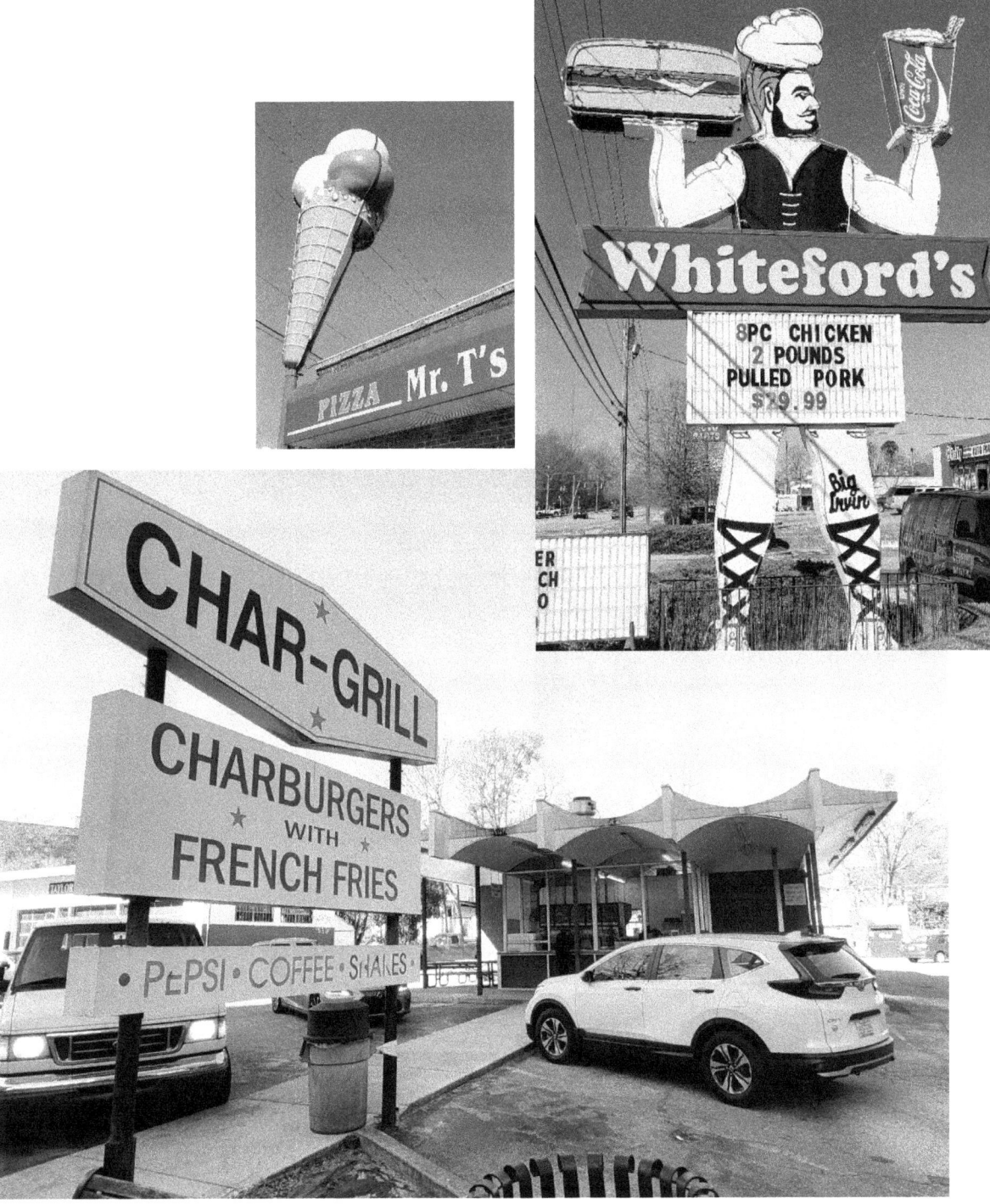

Clockwise from top left: Ice cream cone on Mr. T's Pizza in Chattanooga; Whiteford's on the U.S. 76 bypass in Laurens, S.C., where you can actually buy a BBQ sundae; Char-Grill in downtown Raleigh, N.C. has been in serving burgers since 1959. *Author photos*

Left: Burgers Shakes on New Circle Road in Lexington, Ky., served burgers for 19 cents when it opened in 1957. In 2021, they cost $1.23. *Author photo*

Above: A diner on U.S. 1 in Maryland, 1940. Jack Delano, Library of Congress.
Right: Tanner's Big Orange started out in downtown Greenville, S.C., as the Orange Mill in 1943 and moved to its current location on U.S. 291 when it was a two-lane road in 1966. At one time, it served 2,000 sandwiches a day at Donaldson AFB. *Author photo*

Not all fast-food restaurants offered drive-in service, and not all specialized in chicken or pork. Old-fashioned burgers were popular, too, and a chain called Krystal served them up with a twist: They were square. And small.

At just one ounce, with steamed-in onions, they were a far cry from a Quarter Pounder.

These "sliders" cost just a nickel. There was a reason for this: Co-founder J. Glenn Sherrill said he couldn't charge 10 cents for a hamburger, and other small hamburger stands in the area said they couldn't get that much. Making them small just made sense (five cents, to be exact).

Still, Krystal's slogan invited customers to "take along a sackful."

The outlet's first customer, French C. Jenkins, did just that: He ordered six of them to go with a cup of coffee for a grand total of 35 cents.

Krystal was the South's answer to White Castle, and in fact, co-founder Rody Davenport spent time in Chicago studying the White Castle model. One of the place's hallmarks was cleanliness, so Davenport's wife supposedly suggested the name after seeing a crystal ball lawn decoration; she conceived of it as a signature for "crystal clean" or "clean as a crystal."

Cleanliness was, in fact, one of the restaurant's hallmarks.

"Back in those days, sanitation and cleanliness was questionable," said Gordon Davenport, Rody's son, who served as chairman of the company's executive committee. "This was a place where you knew you weren't in danger of being poisoned."

The first Krystal was a small, 10-stool building (just 10 by 25 feet) in Chattanooga, Tennessee, that was built of steel and porcelain enamel. The prefabricated, box-shaped structure was made in Chicago, then shipped south. On opening day in October 1932, the *Chattanooga News* described it as a "unique eating place" and announced that "a large crowd visited it during the day."

Rody Davenport died in 1943, and Sherrill ran the company after that; Rody Davenport III became president when Sherrill passed away in 1961.

In the 1950s, Krystal followed the trend toward drive-ins, with curbside service in the suburbs, but it proved to be a passing phase. "We built a lot of those, with carhops, the whole nine miles," Gordon Davenport told the Associated Press in 1983. "We don't have any left, thank God. They really made us in the '50s, but they tended to draw a non-family, motorcycle-gang, God-knows-what crowd. They were tough and they hurt our image."

Below: Newspaper ad from March 6, 1933, announcing opening of the second Krystal. Note the slight change in design, with corner door.

Photos: Krystal sign outside Huntsville, Ala., top, and a modern Krystal in Scottsboro, Ala., right, in 2021. *Author photos*

Roy's in Rossville, Ga., opened as the third Krystal location, and the first in Georgia, in 1934. It was torn down and rebuilt at its present site in 1948, when U.S. 27 was widened. *Author photos*

Krystal has a couple of ties to the music world: Elvis Presley apparently loved the place, and it inspired the stage name of country singer Crystal Gayle. Paul "Bear" Bryant, the legendary University of Alabama football coach, liked it, too, and even made a commercial for Krystal.

By the 1980s, Krystal was outselling McDonald's in Tennessee. The chain reached a peak of 420 restaurants in 2002. After some downsizing, there were 291 locations in nine states as of 2021, with Georgia (104) and Tennessee (77) having the most. Other Krystals could be found in Alabama, Florida, and Mississippi, with a handful in South Carolina and Kentucky, a couple in Louisiana, and one in Arkansas.

It's the oldest hamburger chain in the South, and one of the 10 oldest in the country, the first being White Castle. But the two chains only compete with each other in two markets: Kentucky and Nashville.

A Real Hole in the Wall

Krystal wasn't the only fast-food restaurant that Elvis liked. According to one legend, he had a box of jelly doughnuts from Krispy Kreme within reach at all times.

Vernon Rudolph was just 18 years old when he left school in 1933 after a year of college to work at his uncle's general store in Paducah, Kentucky. Ishmael Armstrong sold a little bit of everything there, including doughnuts, which were made with a secret recipe from New Orleans he'd purchased from a pastry chef named Joe LeBoeuf.

When he met Armstrong, LeBoeuf lived in Louisville and was working as a cook on a barge plying the Ohio River. He'd made a name for himself with those doughnuts (along with his pancakes and coconut cakes), and Armstrong must have liked them enough to ask him for the recipe. Maybe he bought it, or maybe LeBoeuf just shared it because he liked it so much.

Either way, LeBoeuf could only make a few dozen doughnuts a day on a river boat, so it wasn't as though he could make a lot of money from them.

Armstrong didn't plan to, either. He brought the recipe back to his store and simply added doughnuts to the list of things he sold there.

Rudolph, though, must have realized they were good enough to serve as the main attraction, because he opened his own doughnut shop in Paducah shortly after that. In order to turn a profit, though, he may have changed the recipe a tad. The exact ingredients remained a secret: The company even locked the recipe away in a vault at its headquarters. But Rudolph's son, Carver, told the Duke University *Chronicle* in 2003 that he and a historian had deduced that it included fluffed egg whites, sugar, mashed potatoes, shortening, skim milk, and (of course) cream.

The blend was mixed with flour, fried and covered in glaze. But you couldn't mass-produce them that way, Carver Rudolph said, so his father must have done something a little differently: "I'm sure he doctored it right away... the proportions just don't work out the same."

He must have found some success, because in 1934, he convinced his uncle to sell the general store and go into business with him selling doughnuts in a bigger market, Nashville. Business was so good that Rudolph's father, Plumie, quit his job digging ditches to join them. A year later, Rudolph's uncle went back to Kentucky, but Rudolph kept working with his father in Nashville for the next two years and even helped another uncle open a shop in Charleston, West Virginia.

There was, evidently, a shop in Decatur, Illinois, as well: A small ad in the *Decatur Daily Review* printed in November 1935 touted "DELICIOUS KRISPY KREME DONUTS — Hot, nightly, 5 to 11."

But was it the same Krispy Kreme? It's hard to know.

More on that in a bit.

Then, in 1937, Rudolph split from his father and decided to move his doughnut enterprise again. He had a particular site scoped out, and had a lease ready to sign, but he noticed there was a lot of competition there and, while he was considering the deal, happened to notice a pack of Camel cigarettes that mentioned Winston-Salem on the label.

That did it. Instead of signing the lease, he headed out of town with a doughnut cutter and a salesman, bound for Winston-Salem.

Whatever his reasons for locating there, it was a natural choice. The city had just incorporated in 1913 as a combination of two nearby towns: Salem, settled before the Revolutionary War, and nearby Winston, named for a local hero who fought in that war, Joseph Winston.

R.J. Reynolds had opened a tobacco factory there in 1875, and scores of other tobacco companies followed suit — almost 40 of them. But it was Reynolds who dominated the industry, buying out his main competitor, Pleasant Henderson Hanes, at the turn of the century. He only solidified his standing when he started selling Camel cigarettes in 1913. Winston-Salem incorporated that same year, and it imported so much Turkish tobacco and French cigarette paper to make Camels that the U.S. government designated it as a port of entry, even though it was 200 miles from the Atlantic Coast.

By 1918, the Reynolds company owned 121 buildings in Winston-Salem, and by the 1940s, more than 60 percent of the city residents worked for either Reynolds or Hanes Textiles. (The company, later famous for its panty hose, had been founded by the same P.H. Hanes who Reynolds had bought out years earlier.)

With nearly 50,000 residents, the tobacco industry had made Winston-Salem the largest city in North Carolina by 1920, and it grew to more than 75,000 by the end of the decade. It was the biggest stop on the road from Washington, D.C., to Atlanta, so there would be plenty of customers to buy Vernon Rudolph's doughnuts.

Rudolph was still just 22 years old when he used his last $25 to lease an 18-foot-wide space in Old Salem, across from Salem College, to make them. He didn't have any money left for ingredients, so he persuaded a local grocer to give him what he needed in exchange for payment once he'd sold his first batch. He continued to work with grocers after that; he didn't even have a shop at first, but sold his creations to them as a way to pull in customers. He made deliveries in a Pontiac he'd driven to Winston-Salem, removing the back seat to make room for the doughnuts.

But being across from the college, the area drew a lot of pedestrians who came walking by his small factory. When passers-by caught the scent of what he was making, they started asking him whether they could buy from him. So, improvising, he cut a hole in the wall of his little factory and started selling them directly to folks right there on the street.

Talk about a hole in the wall.

Customers could look through that hole at the doughnuts being made, and anyone who came by between midnight and 4 in the morning could get 'em while they were hot. As he opened more stores, glass was installed in serving areas so customers could continue to see the doughnut-making process. Like most doughnuts, they were best when hot and fresh, so the company eventually started installing signs that lit up when they were ready, announcing that they were "Hot Now!"

But there was, apparently, another Krispy Kreme in the proverbial mix. In January 1938 *Atlanta Constitution* reported a lease to the "Krispy-Kreme Do-Nut Company," and later that same month, a company by that name announced it was opening a shop in West Asheville, North Carolina, just a few hours west of Winston-Salem. Intriguingly, however,

HIGHWAYS OF THE SOUTH

Vernon Rudolph's name was nowhere in the report. Instead, the company was said to be managed by one L.A. Renison and to have originated in Little Rock, Arkansas, in 1930 — three years *before* Rudolph got into the business.

A 1938 report in the *Asheville Citizen-Times* said that Renison's company had "numerous branches in the east and middle-west that are expanding into many southern states." The "do-nuts" had been recommended by the State Hospital in Little Rock; they contained no animal fat and were cooked in the finest vegetable shortenings, made fresh nearly every two hours from early morning to late evening.

Another branch of this same company opened in Charlotte, also in 1938.

It just so happens that the Renison name is connected with another doughnut business with a very similar name: Crispie Creme of Chillicothe, Ohio. A 2004 article in the *Columbus Dispatch* shed some light on the possible connection: It contained an interview with Mike Renison, who said his grandfather, Jack, had started a Crispie Crème shop in Mulberry, Kansas, back in 1929, but had sold it two years later and moved on.

"Here's what would happen," Mike Renison told the *Chillicothe Gazette* in 2016. "They would start it up and it would go like gangbusters for like the first year, year-and-a-half, and then it would slow down because doughnuts were a fad. Back then, they were."

So his grandfather "kept moving east, and they ended up going into Chicago and he had quite a few shops in Chicago. Again, he would open them up, run them for a year or so, and then he would sell them and move on." Other stops included Indiana and Ohio, where Renison finally settled down in Portsmouth, about 45 miles from Chillicothe. (It was there that Jack Renison's son, James, opened that city's original Crispie Creme shop in 1952.) But before Jack Renison got there, he stopped in Paducah, Kentucky — the same place Ishmael Armstrong ran his general store.

Renison opened a doughnut shop there in 1931, but he sold it two years later.

The buyer, according to the *Dispatch* article, was none other than Vernon Rudolph.

Jack's brother, Lloyd A. Renison, opened his Asheville doughnut shop in 1938 under the Krispy Kreme name. He kept operating that store until at least 1948.

Meanwhile, Rudolph's Krispy Kreme company was growing by leaps and bounds: By the 1950s, it had 29 locations in a dozen states, and had grown to more than 1,000 shops by 2018.

And what about Crispie Creme? It's still open in Chillicothe, Ohio.

Above: Krispy Kreme on U.S. Highway 31E (Bardstown Road) south of Louisville. *Author photo*

Right: Coupon for Krispy Kreme Donuts that appeared in the Muncie Star of Indiana on Dec. 8, 1938.

Motels and More

Colony House Motor Lodge on old U.S. 220 at the south end of Roanoke, Va., offered thoroughly modern accommodations, including an outdoor pool, when it opened in 1957. It looked much the same when it closed in 2018 and was vacant when this photo was taken in 2020. *Author photo*

Plum Tuckered Out

If you're on the road for any length of time, you'll need a place to stop for the night. But where? In the era of the railroad, there weren't many options. You got off the train and checked into a downtown hotel.

With the advent of the automobile and the development of highways, a number of other options opened up. At first, there weren't many places to stop between cities, and with the nation's most popular car — the Model T — topping out at 40 or 45 miles per hour, you often couldn't get to the next town on roads that were far from perfect in a single day. Your only real option was to stop by the roadside and camp out... which is exactly what a lot of people did in the late 1910s and early '20s.

Auto camping actually became a fad, as so-called "tin can tourists" hopped in their cars with tents they pitched by the side of the road whenever the sun began to set: in farmers' fields, beneath billboards, or wherever they could find a clear spot. Tents, bedding, camp stoves, and other merchandise began selling briskly. In 1924, one retailer even sponsored a national contest for students to choose the best essay on "Why Auto Camping Has Become a Popular Recreation."

Winning essay from the 1924 contest

Auto-camping provides the inexpensiveness, independence, and comfort desired by the average American family in traveling.

The call of the out-of-doors influences many to decide on auto tours, because these mean health and happiness for all.

Well-equipped tourist camps, good roads, auto maps, and modern camp equipment — tents, auto-beds, improved camp stoves, etc., have all made auto-camping a popular recreation.

Besides the enjoyment derived from these trips, there comes to the auto camper a better realization of the greatness of the United States, its wonderful resources and beautiful scenery. The educational advantages of auto-camping offer great inducements to travelers.

Margaret Schrubbe of Decorah, Iowa, winner of $100

Early "snowbirds" flocked to sunny Florida, fleeing the Midwest snows in winter and heading South on the Dixie Highway, a project spearheaded by Indy 500 raceway builder Carl Fisher — who also happened to be a major Miami land developer.

The highway, which hit the drawing board in 1914, was a north-south sequel to Fisher's transcontinental Lincoln Highway. But the name "highway" was a misnomer, because it was actually a loop that incorporated several different roads and offered two main parallel paths south. One from Chicago via Indianapolis, Louisville, Nashville, and Atlanta, and the other came down from Detroit down through Ohio, eastern Kentucky and Tennessee, the Carolinas and Jacksonville.

There were several connecting roads and secondary alternates in the Dixie Highway network, as well, but the point of it all was to give road-trippers a way to escape the cold and spend their winters (and money) in the South.

How successful was this enterprise? In 1923, *The Jacksonville Observer* crowed that early birds were already on their way in late September:

"They are coming. The advance guard is already here. Scores of automobiles from other states passed through Jacksonville this week. They were headed for St. Petersburg and other South Florida points."

The newspaper suggested converting the state fairgrounds into a giant auto camp and allowing tourists to use the buildings for "dances, lectures, and other amusements."

The business opportunities were obvious: "By January 1st there should be at least 2,000 tourists in camp and there would be if the proper action is taken. These tourists would give Jacksonville thousands of dollars' worth of advertising. Many of them are well provided with funds and some would be induced to invest in Duval county lands. They would buy supplies from our merchants and be valuable in every way."

Jacksonville wasn't alone. A number of cities started opening auto camps on the outskirts of town, seeking to keep road-trippers close enough to capture their tourist dollars. And entrepreneurs weren't far behind, clearing land so they could charge a fee for a place to set up a tent, and perhaps some running water and a communal toilet.

The auto camping craze began to wane as the 1920s wore on, and the Florida tourist boom took a huge hit in 1926, when the Great Miami Hurricane devastated South Florida, causing $100 million in damage. Even so, the trend spawned a pair of industries that would continue to evolve over the years to come: the motel and the RV park.

Motels didn't get their name until 1925, when the Milestone Mo-Tel opened in San Luis Obispo, California, but even then, they didn't often go by that name. Early motels replaced tents with basic cottages, often arrayed around a central courtyard — hence the name "auto court" or "motor court," the latter being the most popular in the 1930s and '40s.

The Rainbow Autel was built in the mid-1950s along U.S. Highway 11 in Chilhowie, Va. With a restaurant and nearby Texaco service station, it offered free TV and telephones in every room, room service, and air conditioning. The autel no longer exists, but the sign was salvaged and survives at a storage facility up the road. *Author photo*

Other establishments branded themselves as tourist courts, motor lodges, or even "autels." *The Newport News Daily Press* in Virginia described any such business as "a group of buildings containing individual sleeping units, designed for or used temporarily by tourists or transients, with garage or parking space conveniently located to each unit." Cooking facilities, it added, were sometimes provided.

In the late 1930s, motor courts started to band together in associations to provide quality assurance to their patrons. These referral groups weren't chains, but they produced guidebooks and brochures that gave travelers an idea of where to find "approved" motels that were part of the group. This was especially helpful to vacationers in the Great Depression, when a growing number of transients took up residence in old auto camps and cottages.

United Courts, founded in the Southwest in 1933, started the trend, followed in 1939 by Quality Courts United (which became an actual chain, Quality Inn, in the 1960s.) Best Western, founded in 1946, also began as a referral operation, identifying the best motor lodges in Western states.

Above: Old motel cabins sit abandoned in February 2021 along U.S. 220 south of Rocky Mount, Va. *Author photo*

Left: Cotton Boll Court in the "Heart of the Delta," Clarksdale, Miss., in October 1939. *Marion Post Wolcott, Library of Congress*

Quality Courts started out with seven motels in Florida and by 1945 had expanded its service area across nine Southern states, plus a single motel in Gettysburg, Pennsylvania. Its booklet that year provided detailed half-page entries on properties from the Moon-Winx Court in Tuscaloosa, Alabama to the Carolynne Tourist Court in Williamsburg, Virginia.

(Of the guide book's 51 entries, more than half contained the word "court" or "courts," while there were about seven "cottages." The word "motel" was nowhere to be found.)

Superior Courts, founded in 1950, featured a four-leaf clover logo and served much the same region, covering the South Atlantic states, from Maryland down to Florida. Many of the properties were along U.S. Highway 1.

A Superior Courts brochure in March of 1952 described the advantages of the referral system:

"It is often difficult to know which court will please you without stopping to look them over, but this takes much time and effort when you are tired. This list of courts has been prepared to help you avoid this uncertainty. Every one of them has been selected because of the unusual excellence of its accommodations and services, and you may rest assured that you will find the comfort, cleanliness, and courtesy that will make you want to come again and to recommend SUPERIOR COURTS to your friends."

Circle Courts in Waco, Texas, offered modern "apartments for tourists" on Highway 81 at "The Circle" in November of 1939. The big 200-foot roundabout, the oldest in Texas, was built in 1935 was where U.S. 81 (since replaced by Interstate 35) and U.S. 77 converged heading north toward Dallas. It caused plenty of confusion, leading some entrepreneurs to produce T-shirts bearing the message "I survived the circle." A giant lone star was added to the center of the circle in 2013. *Lee Russell, Library of Congress*

Above: Front and back covers of Quality Courts United's 1945 travel guide. *Author collection*
Below: Cabins on U.S. 80, the Dallas-Fort Worth Highway, in January 1942. *Arthur Rothstein, Library of Congress*

Grogan's Tourist Court on U.S. 311/220 in Madison, N.C., opened in 1931 but has long been abandoned. Owned by Mr. and Mrs. C.E. Grogan, it offered a restaurant across the street, with amenities that included (in 1941) steam heat, free locked garages, private baths with showers, and Simmons beds. *Author photos*

Early motor courts were often built quickly to take advantage of the travel boom in the 1920s. Many cabins were hastily erected wooden structures that weren't built to last, so the owners either rebuilt them (if they were profitable) with sturdier materials, or sold them to others (if they weren't). Some were torn down, while others became cheap housing for low-income residents.

A few old wooden cabins can still be seen, in various states of disrepair along Southern highways, but most of them are gone. Some early entrepreneurs, however, built their roadside inns to last. One example is the stone-and-plaster Grogan Tourist Courts along old U.S. 220 just outside Madison in North Carolina. The building on the Dan River, with its small, distinctive faux gables, dates back to around 1930, and is the most intact early motel in Rockingham County. The central section of the motel complex was built first, with expansions in the 1930s and again — without garages this time — in the '50s.

There was also a restaurant across the street that opened around the same time as the tourist court. In 1939, it offered a 35-cent meal that included a serving of meat, four veggies, a drink, and dessert. The place catered to a variety of customers, from tourist court guests to tobacco farmers. In 1945, the Madison High School held a sophomore-senior banquet there, according to the *Madison Messenger*. It was the only such banquet ever held, because there was no junior class that year: North Carolina had just added the 12th grade:

"The sophomores hosted the event and decorated the venue with their class colors of green and white," the newspaper reported. "At the banquet held on a Friday night at Grogan's Restaurant located just east of the bridge entering the town of Madison, attendees dined by candlelight, heard toasts to the seniors and faculty, and enjoyed a musical program."

The county medical society held a meeting there in 1954 to discuss Jonas Salk's polio vaccine.

The back of the west building of Grogan's Tourist Court, with the office in the foreground in February 2021. Renovations were under way when this photo was taken, with new doors among the improvements already made. *Author photo*

Above: The old restaurant building at Grogan's was across the main highway.

Right: One of the tourist court's built-in garages. *Author photos*

Horseshoe Camp, Bowling Green, Kentucky

If you travel south on U.S. Route 31W from Cave City, Ky., you'll come across the ruin of Horseshoe Camp, a stone structure like Grogan's that dates from roughly the same era: the 1930s. Four of the buildings were constructed from limestone dug of from nearby quarries.

The office building, pictured here, had a gas pump out front and also housed a beer tavern, gift shop, and three cottage units. The "modern cottages" with attached garages featured pine paneling, tile floors, a double bed, rocking chair, straight chair, and dressing table with a mirror. There were eight buildings, including an owner's residence. The motel closed sometime in the early 1970s.

Unfortunately, a fire gutted most of the property in 2014, although the stone frames and some of the green-and-white metal awnings survived. The sign was spared, as well, although it provides a clue to the ill fortune that visited the place in the end: All the luck had run out of the upside-down horseshoe. *Author photo*

Unlike many motor courts, which provided open parking spaces or covered carports for their guests, garages at Grogan's were built right into one long structure, which housed the rooms together, rather than in separate cottages. This allowed for an extra level of privacy that attracted those who desired it for discreet rendezvous, making it one of the early "no tell motels." The proprietors would open the garages for visitors before their arrival, giving them direct access to rooms that included a bed with a Red Cross mattress, wooden dresser, and a round table with shaded lamp.

Grogan's, like many early motor courts, was a family-owned "mom and pop" operation rather than a chain. Most tourist courts of the time were. At Ring's Rest in Maryland, owner Fred Ringe's children pitched in to help greet guests, make up the rooms, and pump gas. Ringe purchased the modest four-cabin setup with store and gas pumps on U.S. Highway 1 in 1934, about four years after it opened as the Lone Pine Inn. The cabins didn't have their own facilities; you had to use an outhouse. And they didn't allow local guests: Cottages were already developing a reputation in the 1920s as dens of iniquity.

Colonial Cottages outside Louisville, Ky., tried to fend off the bad reputation associated with tourist courts and cottages by posting a sign that kept locals from checking in. The cottages were "strictly tourist" when this photo was taken in July of 1940. *Marion Post Wolcott, Library of Congress*

As early as 1925, FBI Director J. Edgar Hoover had warned that tourist cabins were "hotbeds of crime" that attracted hoodlums, who used them as hideouts.

Hotel owners stoked such rumors in an attempt to curb the competition. But there was a certain logic to them: Tourist cabins were close to the highway, offering easy access along with privacy. Rooms could be rented on the cheap, which made them magnets for drifters and grifters.

By 1939, ten states had passed laws that required tourist camps to obtain some form of license. Arkansas required that "auto camps" keep a record of guests' names and addresses; that the health and safety of guests be protected; and that the camps be operated "in a law-abiding manner."

North Carolina went further, requiring all cabin camps and tourist camps to keep a register of license plate numbers, in addition to names and addresses. Anyone who occupied a room "for immoral purposes" would be guilty of a misdemeanor, and operators who knew about it would be, too. Health inspections would be conducted, and a violation of any provision in the statute could result in fines. Or imprisonment.

But the days of the auto camp and cabin courts were already fading. Courts with separate cabins soon gave way to motel complexes with many rooms housed in a single building, similar to hotels. But they tended to spread out, ranch-style, over one or two stories — often with external walkways — rather than vertically with interior corridors.

One standout example of this was Boots Court Motel on Route 66 in Carthage, Missouri. Built in 1939 in an art-deco style with rounded corners that made it look a little like a giant icebox, Boots was at the highway's intersection with U.S. 71, which wound up north from Baton Rouge all the way to the Canadian border at International Falls, Minnesota.

Carthage, near Joplin and just north of the Arkansas state line, was at an important intersection, and so was Boots. In fact, it was sometimes referred to as the "Crossroads of America." Clark Gable stayed there a number of times, choosing Room No. 6

The motel, named for founder Arthur Boots, offered a radio in each of its 14 rooms in the days before TV, along with tile showers, floor furnaces with thermostat control, air conditioning and a garage. (Televisions were, in fact, added later, along with Beautyrest mattresses — which many motels touted.) It attracted visitors with green neon lighting that rimmed the structure above the doors. There was also a similarly styled Boots Drive-in and Gift Shop, across the street, which opened in 1946 and operated until 1970.

The place changed its name slightly along the way to Boots Motel and added an awkward-looking gabled roof, but new owners bought it in 2011 and restored its original name and appearance.

Right: The Boots Court neon sign, on Route 66 at U.S. 71, had been refurbished when this photo was taken in the spring of 2019 to look the way it did in 1949. It boasts that it's air conditioned and features a "radio in every room."

Below: The Boots Court office in 2019, with the same kind of chairs out front that are visible in vintage postcard photos, but without the window awnings. *Author photos*

Top: Cabins near Bardstown, Ky., 1940. *Marion Post Wolcott, Library of Congress*

Center: 11-70 Motor Court, along shared U.S. routes 11 and 70 in Knoxville, Tenn., in 2019. *Author photo*

Bottom: Trav O Tel in Corpus Christie, Texas in 1939. *Lee Russell, Library of Congress*

The Windsor Village Motel occupied a prime spot at the intersection of U.S. 31 and U.S. 64 in Pulaski, Tenn. Built sometime in the 1930s, it offered "Tourist Cottages De Luxe," in 29 rooms that were "full for days" with snowbound tourists in late January 1948. The motel manager had to find space in local homes for 75 guests he couldn't accommodate.

By 2021, though, the motel was far from its glory days, as seen here. Some of the larger buildings, which were originally built as garages, are now rooms. *Author photos*

A Tale of Two Chains

As the years passed, independently owned motels gradually gave way to larger chains, the first of which was Texas-based Alamo Plaza Courts, which opened as the Alamo Plaza Tourist Apartments in Waco, Texas, in 1929. The façade, designed (naturally) to look like the Alamo was replicated across the South. Owner Edgar Lee Torrance added his second location — a $60,000 complex — in Tyler two years later.

Despite the "tourist" name, it was clear that Torrance was marketing his business to locals seeking a permanent living situation. On the eve of the Tyler location's opening, he took out a full-page ad in the *Courier-Times* promoting the Courts, and noting that some units contained as many as four rooms, foreshadowing the modern suite hotel.

The Alamo units were, according to the *Tyler Morning Telegraph*, "furnished with every convenience," making them "the ideal place to live." Weekly rates for permanent residents were $15, and rooms came equipped with hardwood floors, a gas stove, double bed, day bed, breakfast set, writing table, chairs, draperies "and everything that is found in a modern home." A few years later, in 1936, Alamo Plaza became one of the first motels to install telephones in every room.

Torrance didn't want anything to do with locals interested in renting by the hour.

"We cater to tourists and traveling salesmen," he said. "We don't admit couples with local driver's licenses."

Torrance built a third location in Shreveport in 1935, and others followed. More than 30 of locations were operating in a dozen states at one time or another, all of them in the South, except for one in Indianapolis that didn't use the classic Alamo architecture. A location in Raleigh, North Carolina, was the farthest from the chain's Texas base.

Almost all of the Alamo Plazas were on the original federal highway network, which meant the chain suffered when the interstate system began to bypass its locations in the late 1950s. That's when the chain decided on a "complete change-over." It dropped the historic façade for a more modern look; it tried to grab motorists' attention by installing massive neon signs featuring a giant "A" surmounted by a star; and it changed its name again — to Alamo Plaza *Hotel* Courts. A franchise plan was launched in 1959, then discontinued a year later after 50 sites had signed on, and the chain went downhill after that, overtaken by competitors. One, in particular.

Top: Alamo Plaza's first location, in Waco, seen in June 1939. *Don O'Brien, Creative Commons 2.0*

Above: A Texas competitor, Mission Courts, on the Dallas-Fort Worth Highway (U.S. 80) in January 1942. *Arthur Rothstein, Library of Congress*

HIGHWAYS OF THE SOUTH

While Alamo Plaza may have been the first major chain of motor courts, it was hardly the most successful. In fact, the franchise concept and big neon sign it adopted at the end of the 1950s were both attempts to duplicate the success of another chain that had begun in the South two decades after Alamo Plaza had built its first motel. But in a few short years, that chain had gone from a startup to an 800-pound gorilla in the hospitality industry.

That chain was Holiday Inn, named after the 1942 Bing Crosby Christmas movie. Actually, it started off being called Holiday Inn Hotel Courts (Alamo Plaza would copy the "hotel courts" language in its rebranding initiative, in addition to the rival chain's Great Sign.).

Kemmons Wilson was already a successful developer from Memphis by the time he got into the motel business. He'd built 40 commercial buildings, 700 single-family homes and an apartment house since World War II when a new idea hit him. Embarking on a trip to Washington, D.C., he found himself disappointed with the quality of the roadside inns he encountered along the way. He realized travelers wanted "clean, roomy rooms, with good all-tile baths and air conditioning at a reasonable price."

But price couldn't be the only factor, or quality would suffer. Accordingly, Wilson decided to target "the carriage trade, the Cadillac trade," which got him thinking about added features. Many motels were already built alongside restaurants, but what about gift shops where visitors could watch as the staff produced freshly made pralines? Other possibilities included house physicians, babysitting services, kennels for traveling dogs, and airport pick-up service. Why not a barbershop and a valet on top of that?

There was no better place to start his experiment than Memphis, where not a single new hotel room had been built since 1929, even though the city had doubled in size since then. Hotels were expensive to build, at about $12,000 a room, but high-end motels could be built for less than half that price: about $5,000 per room.

"I figured the motel business was the greatest untouched business in the country," Wilson said. "I studied everything I could find on motels (in) trade magazines and articles, (and) visited 100 different ones. I talked to people who stayed at them and people who ran them, found out what made them tick. Then I got my own architect, and we drew one like we thought it ought to be — we've changed every one since."

Wilson quickly built four Holiday Inns, each along a U.S. highway at a different corner of city. The first one was on the east side, along U.S. 79, which led to Nashville. The second went up along U.S. 51 South, heading toward Jackson, Mississippi, and another was built on the same road heading north to Kentucky and Illinois. There was also one on Route 61 — the same road featured in the title of Bob Dylan's album *Highway 61 Revisited* — which went southwest before turning south toward New Orleans.

This last one was the fourth to be built: a 129-unit motel catering to convention-goers. It included a ballroom and convention hall that seated 500 people, as well as a pair of private dining rooms dubbed the Caribbean Room and Holiday Room. But Wilson was just getting started.

Holiday Inns in 1956

ALABAMA
Auburn*
Birmingham
Huntsville*
Mobile*
Montgomery*

ARKANSAS
Pine Bluff

ARIZONA
Flagstaff*

COLORADO
Colorado Springs

GEORGIA
Macon*

KANSAS
Great Bend*
Kansas City*
Lawrence*
Mission*
Salina*
Topeka*
Wichita

LOUISIANA
Alexandria
Lafayette*
Monroe*

MISSISSIPPI
Clarksdale
Greenwood
Hattiesburg
Jackson*
Long Beach*
Meridian*

MISSOURI
Kansas City
St. Louis*

NEW MEXICO
Albuquerque*

N. CAROLINA
Greensboro

OKLAHOMA
Oklahoma City
Tulsa*

OHIO
Canton*
Toledo*

S. CAROLINA
Charleston
Myrtle Beach*

TENNESSEE
Jackson
Knoxville*
Memphis (East)
Memphis (North)
Memphis (South)
Memphis (West)

TEXAS
Amarillo
Dallas*

*Planned or under construction

He already had dreams of expanding beyond Memphis: Shortly after he began building, he hosted a group of 65 millionaires at his Holiday Inn South to pitch a franchise system that he hoped would involve 69 motels in 28 states.

It eventually got a lot bigger than that.

A 1956 directory showed 21 locations in 13 states, all but two of them (in Colorado Springs and Wichita) in the South. Tennessee and Mississippi had five each, and the chain stretched east all the way to Portsmouth, Virginia.

But the same directory also showed big plans for expansion, with more locations on the drawing boards. Rooms ran for $5 or $6 for a single, a dollar or two more for a double, and suites for $10 to $12 "in keeping with the nation-wide Holiday Inn Pattern of superior accommodations at moderate cost."

One of the four first Holiday Inns, on U.S. 61 South, in the 1950s. *Author collection*

Holiday Inn had an advantage on Alamo Plaza and other older motels because it came along just about the time the new interstate system was about to be built. Those earlier businesses had been built along the federal highway system, but those roads through town were about to be bypassed by President Eisenhower's interstates. Property for new Holiday Inns was often purchased at interstate off-ramps, giving motorists ideal access.

It wasn't long before Holiday Inn started living up to its motto, "Your host from coast to coast." By 1965, the chain had 500 in operation and 200 more in the works, covering 44 states. That was the same year Alamo Plaza opened its final motel, on U.S. 80 in

Shreveport, Louisiana. It simply couldn't keep up. (The Shreveport motel later changed its name to Alamo Inn, and finally became a Travelodge.)

Holiday Inn didn't just operate roadside motels, but had city-center hotels, too boot. The 50-foot-tall "Great Sign" was phased out in 1982. The first one had cost $13,000, and they were just too expensive.

The Holiday Inn sign had evolved slightly by the 1960s, dropping the "Hotel Courts" name and rebranding the chain as "Holiday Inns of America." This one is seen along U.S. Highway 90 in Mobile, Ala. *Author collection*

Other chains didn't start in the South but also had a presence there. Howard Johnson's, which got its start in New England serving up ice cream, expanded into a large chain of diner-type eateries and added hotels alongside them.

By 1966, it had 285 motor lodges in 36 states, plus the District of Columbia and the Bahamas. About 4 in 10 of those were in the South, including 47 in Florida alone. Central offices in Atlanta and another in Miami took reservations around the clock. "Adjacent to each motor lodge, you will always find the familiar orange roof — our restaurants — which assures you of one-stop convenience at all times," Johnson wrote in the 1966 directory.

Ironically, the restaurants went out of business, but many of the lodges remain.

Does the Star Lite Motel sign on U.S. 52 in Mount Airy, N.C. look familiar? It should, because it looks a lot like a Holiday Inn sign. Whether it is or not is an interesting question, because the Star Lite has been operating under that name since the 1960s, when a postcard touted its "twenty new, modern units." By contrast, there was no Holiday Inn in Mount Airy as of 1962. The sign is seen here in 2020, minus the original lights and neon. *Author photos*

Holiday Inn hardly had a monopoly on the Great Sign concept, as these photos illustrate. *Author photos*

Left: The similarly named Holiday Motel is one of several on the U.S. 31W strip in Cave City, a popular destination for the underground caverns nearby.

Below: The Sugar -n- Spice Drive-In has been operating on State Route 9 in Spartanburg, S.C., since 1961.

More recent motels from the 1950s onward show how architecture evolved but retained some elements used in an earlier era. *Author photos*

Top: A former Howard Johnson's motel on U.S. 1 in Rockingham, N.C., was built in an L shape that retained echoes of the former courtyard model. **Above:** Gables on a Budget Inn in Madison, N.C., preserve the look of individual cottages, even though rooms are contained in a single building. The motel, which sits on the modern U.S. 220 alignment, probably dates to no earlier than 1963, when that highway bypassed an earlier alignment through downtown Madison to the west.

Above: An abandoned Howard Johnson's restaurant sits across from the motel seen on the previous page in Rockingham, N.C. *Author photo*

Left: A Howard Johnson's ad touting its menu of "full-course meals, salads, sandwiches and tempting desserts. *Author collection*

As highways got bigger, signs did, too.

Above: The Scotland Inn on U.S. 401 in Laurinburg, N.C.; photo from February 2021.

Right: A massive falling-apart motel sign on Route 66 in Villa Ridge, Mo., seen in 2019.
Author photos

The Mountaineer Inn in Asheville, N.C., was built in 1948 as the 19-unit Mountaineer Court, and 44 units were added in 1973. A newspaper ad in 1952 touted its "radios, cedar closets and paneling, wall-to-wall carpets (and) tile bath combinations." The motel on U.S. Highway 70, seen in 2020, features a distinctive rifle-toting barefoot hillbilly on its main sign, along with a neon Popeye on the roof. *Author photos*

The double-decker "Gypsy Van" that Roland Conklin drove from Long Island to California in 1915. *Library of Congress.*

Lodging on Wheels

During the Great Depression, many old auto camps became havens for transients who had no other place to stay. Then, with the start of World War II, a new phenomenon sprang up: the trailer park.

Traveling with trailers wasn't new, even then. The first motorhome, which had a toilet and could sleep up to 11 people, was created in 1910 from a three-ton Packard Truck. Five years later, bus manufacturer Roland Conklin built an eight-ton "Gypsy Van" that contained a kitchen, sleeping berths, convertible sofas, a hidden bookcase, a phonograph and a "roof garden."

In those days, however, most roads couldn't accommodate a behemoth like Conklin's land yacht, and most folks couldn't afford them, anyway. So they purchased tents that could be attached to cars, complete with fold-out beds, which were much more affordable. Unfortunately, they also got soaked in a downpour.

Enter the trailer, which was more expensive but offered dependable shelter from the elements and could be unhitched from the car in case you wanted to leave it somewhere and drive off down a less-welcoming gravel path.

Airstream started building trailers at a small California factory in 1931, but the business didn't really hit its stride for a few years. It was in 1936 that factories began mass-producing them, and economist Roger Babson was so bullish on them that he called them "20th century covered wagons" with "tremendous potential." The following year, there were about 400 companies wheeling them out.

"In brief, I believe that in time half the families who own automobiles will also own trailers," Babson declared.

The future looked bright, but then the war intervened. It wasn't that the effort put a damper on the market for trailers. Just the opposite: It created a massive demand for them. The problem is, manufacturers still hadn't worked all the bugs out by the time the United States entered World War II... and decided it needed a lot of them.

Even before the U.S. entered the war, preparations were being made on the home front. In 1941 alone, the Corps of Engineers built 42 new airfields and housing to go along with them, some of the largest of which were in the South: Keesler Field in Biloxi, Mississippi, and Sheppard Field Wichita Falls, Texas were each designed to house more than 24,000 service members.

A total of 1.5 million military trainees from all over the country descended on Texas, which was suddenly home to 175 installations. Indeed, construction workers were busy building and expanding military bases across the South, many of them in rural areas that needed to provide gas, food, and entertainment along the highway for the workers and, once they'd done their jobs, service members. Fort Bragg, North Carolina, grew from 376 buildings occupied by 5,400 men in the fall of 1940 to about ten times that size — 3,135 buildings housing 67,000 troops — nine months later.

In Mississippi, Ingalls Shipbuilding employed 12,000 men and women, who had built more than 70 ships by 1945. Ammunition plants were built in Flora and Prairie at a cost of $15 million and $25 million respectively. It took more than 7,000 construction workers to build more than 300 buildings at the Prairie plant.

HIGHWAYS OF THE SOUTH

Those and other construction workers involved in the war effort wouldn't be staying permanently, so they needed temporary shelter until their jobs were done. That's where the trailers came in. They'd been designed as an alternative to motor courts for travelers who wanted a little more freedom. But now, they were being used as full-time residences. The government ordered thousands of them to house workers assigned to build and expand military installations, but the workers weren't used to living in them, and the manufacturers had to crank out so many that quality control wasn't always a priority.

Above: This trailer camp in Alexandria, Va., was, occupied mostly by torpedo plant workers in March 1941.

Right: A Good Humor ice cream man delivers treats for workers' kids. *Martha McMillan Roberts, Library of Congress*

Store owner W.T. Mullins rented trailer space on his property near Columbus, Ga., for $2 a week to whoever could afford it. **Top:** Construction worker Paul Knight came from Atlanta to build barracks at Fort Benning. He said the bad roads were one of the worst problems in the area. **Above:** An itinerant photographer was another tenant on Mullins' property. He charged passersby 10 cents for three photos. *Marion Post Wolcott, Library of Congress*

HIGHWAYS OF THE SOUTH

Left: A construction worker and his family were living at a trailer camp in Portsmouth, Va., March 1941. *John Vachon, Library of Congress*

Above: Trailer camps, cabins, liquor, stores, hotels, and other business sprang up for 10 miles on U.S. 71 to serve Camp Crowder in Missouri, where construction began in fall of 1941. This photo was taken by John Vachon in February of 1942. *Library of Congress*

Top: A trailer park and café along U.S. 80, the Dallas-Fort Worth Highway, in January 1942. *Arthur Rothstein, Library of Congress*

Above: Trailer courts and tourist courts sometimes shared the same property, and proprietor, as the Louisiana's Pine View Trailer Court did in December 1940. *Marion Post Wolcott, Library of Congress*

Florida was still a destination for tourist trailers in the late 1930s, as these photos illustrate. **Top:** A trailer camp near Dania, which was described by the photographer as "one of better camps in Florida," charged $5 a week for electricity in January of 1937. *Arthur Rothstein, Library of Congress*

Above: Cottages and a trailer park om the Plant City area, 1939. Marion Post Wolcott, *Library of Congress*

Roger Babson, the economist, had emphasized that "readers must clearly distinguish between the mobile home and the trailer. The trailer is in reality a glorified camping outfit for cruising during pleasant weather. The basic idea behind the trailer is a vehicle made inhabitable. The mobile house, however, is a permanent home made portable."

Those lines, however, had become blurred during wartime and would remain so.

After the war was over, a survey found that trailer coaches were being used to house 1.5 million people — and between 80 and 90 percent of them were being utilized as housing, rather than for travel. Residents included veterans, students and others "who would ordinarily prefer and apartment or house, and who do not intend to take advantage of the mobile features of the house trailer," the survey found. "For the non-mobile person, the trailer is a substitute for a permanent dwelling unit, and the chief advantage of the trailer is its relatively low cost."

At the time of the survey, there were about 8,000 trailer camps nationwide, with large concentrations found in Florida and Texas. But not all were residential. At the other end of the spectrum, an increasingly mobile middle class was clamoring for more RV opportunities. The 1950 survey showed that travel-oriented camps could be found in state parks in 33 states, and 27 national parks had parking sites for trailers.

Motorized RVs were gaining traction, as shown in the 1953 Lucille Ball-Desi Arnaz movie *The Long, Long Trailer*. These luxury models were pricey and out of reach for most families when they first appeared. But Winnebago — founded in 1958 to design furniture for trailers — made the motorhome accessible to more buyers in 1967, when it rolled out "America's first family of motor homes," priced as low as $5,000. The boom of the 1950s and '60s, stoked by postwar prosperity and the new interstate highway system, helped modernize the trailer camp era as RV campground chains, like motel chains, began to dominate the landscape. Kampgrounds of (KOA) was founded in 1962, and the Good Sam Club followed in 1966. Stanley Marcus of Neiman-Marcus even built an upscale prototype in Dallas.

Still, trailers, like motels, continued to be havens for those who couldn't afford better housing. Run-down motels on old highways bypassed by modern interstates were rented weekly or monthly to residents, rather than travelers, and trailers were set up alongside mobile homes at some trailer parks. Other trailer owners set theirs up on land they owned or leased by the side of the road.

HIGHWAYS OF THE SOUTH

Top and center: Al and Roey Stickles have dinner in their trailer at Everglades National Park and walk their baby at Sarasota Trailer Park in 1946.

Below: An Airstream trailer parked at Philips Picnic Area in Florida in 1958.
Florida State Archives

Yogi Bear greets visitors to his Jellystone Park Camp Resort, just west of Cave City, Ky., on State Route 70 to Mammoth Cave. As of 2021, the chain had more than 75 RV parks in the United States and Canada, according to its website. *Author photo*

As time went on, trailers, like motels, lost their luster, and many forgot the integral part they played in opening up the highways of the South to travel. But history shows they provided important stepping stones across the country at a time when the American road was far less smooth, and the vehicles that traveled it were far less reliable than they are today.

Attention Grabbers

A yawning hippo, an ape, and a giant chicken greet motorists along the Donna Fargo Highway in North Carolina. *Author photo*

Made You Look!

If you're on the road, you're bombarded by billboards urging you to buy some product or directing you toward some destination. Then there are just plain peculiar sights that seem to serve no particular purpose beyond a simple, "See? Made you look!"

Neon lights were favorites of motels, casinos, and other businesses, particularly in the middle of the 20th century, when huge arrows directed motorists to "stop here!" The following pages contain some such images from the roadside. I hope you enjoy them, and I hope you've enjoyed this journey down the highways of the South.

Left: A giant pencil points the way to Wytheville Office Supply in Virginia. *Author photo*

Right: A smiling peanut on Highway 49 in Plains, Ga., President Jimmy Carter's hometown. *Mark Harrell, Library of Congress*

HIGHWAYS OF THE SOUTH

Above: Cyborg Muffler Man in Buena Vista, Va.

Left: A more typical Muffler Man, in Paul Bunyan style, on U.S. 11 in Roanoke, Va. *Author photos*

Left: Figure advertises Young Enterprises on Andy Griffith Parkway in Mt. Airy, N.C.

Below: Terminator on U.S. 31W, entering Nashville from the north. *Author photos*

HIGHWAYS OF THE SOUTH

Right and below: The Blue Whale on Route 66 in Oklahoma, 2019. *Author photos*

Carnival on U.S. 1 in Maryland, June 1940. *Jack Delano, Library of Congress*

From top: Mammy's Cupboard on Highway 61 South in Natchez, Miss., and The Pig in Harlingen, Texas, photographed in February 1939 by Lee Russell. *Library of Congress*

Above: One-Spot Flea Killer, in the shape of a dog, off U.S. 1 near Waterloo, Md., in 1940. *Jack Delano, Library of Congress*

Right: Coffee Pot House on U.S. 60 west of Lexington, Va., in 2020. *Author photo*

Left: A hot dog pours ketchup on itself outside a former service station in Reidsville, N.C., that's been converted into a small eatery.

Below: Sign for the Jesse James Wax Museum on Route 66 in Stanton, Mo. *Author photos*

Above: Sign on Texas Tavern in downtown Roanoke, Va., a 10-stool diner which has been in business since the 1930s.

From top: Service station in Waco, Texas, photographed by Lee Russell in November of 1939. Billboards on the Dallas-Ft. Worth Highway in 1942. *Library of Congress*

A pair of vintage signs in Roanoke, Va. The H&C sign used to light up in such a way that it *appeared* coffee was pouring into the cup. *Author photos*

From top: Bull Durham sign in Durham, N.C., 2021. Texas state line sign plastered with stickers in 2019. *Author photos*

From top: A sign advertising 24-hour cleaning in Roanoke, Va. Meadow Gold Milk and Ice Cream sign on Route 66 in Tulsa, Okla. *Author photos*

Above: Bear Wheel Alignment on U.S. 25E in Corbin, Ky. Bear Manufacturing's "Happy Bear" signs first appeared in the 1920s, and the logo was even used by the Grateful Dead. *Author photo*

Above: June 1935 in Reedsville W.V. *Walker Evans, Library of Congress*

Right: An old Kaiser Frazer sign on Route 66 in Missouri, 2019. The car company has been out of business since 1955. *Author photo*

Above: Signs in front of the Hi-Way Tavern, Crystal City, Texas, advertise Coca-Cola, Dr. Pepper, 7Up, Gulf gasoline, Budweiser, and more in March 1939. *Lee Russell, Library of Congress*

Right: Highway marker in Polk County, Fla., winter 1937. *Arthur Rothstein, Library of Congress*

Coke and Pepsi signs on the building walls in downtown Roanoke, Va. *Author photos*

Palm readers have been waving down motorists with painted hands for decades.

Above: On a highway near Fort Benning, Ga., 1940 Marion *Post Wolcott, Library of Congress*

Left: In South Carolina in 2021. *Author photo*

Above: Pal's sports a giant burger, hot dog, fries, and soda on U.S. 58 in western Virginia, one of 30 locations in Tennessee and Virginia as of 2021.

Left: One of the few remaining vintage Arby's neon signs can be found in Danville, Va., on U.S. Business 29. *Author photos*

Above: The Washington Monument rises above Washington, D.C., which was created as the nation's capital after it was decided in 1790 to place the federal district in the Southern United States. The 555-foot marble obelisk was completed in 1884.

Left: The 630-foot Gateway Arch in St. Louis, completed in 1965, is "The Gateway to the West," but could be considered the gateway to the South, as well. *Author photos*

Signs massive and modest.

Above: Welcome sign in Bristol, on the state line between Virginia and Tennessee.

Left: Missy's One Stop in Dillon, S.C. *Author photos*

The Grand Motel on U.S. 1 in South Carolina, 2021. *Author photo*

On a Texas highway north of San Antonio in March of 1940. *Lee Russell, Library of Congress*

Sources

"7-Eleven (Seven & I Holdings) history and history video," companieshistory.com/7-eleven.

"291 Krystal Locations in the United States," locations.krystal.com.

"1947 NASCAR Recap," auto.howstuffworks.com.

"A Car's a Car for a' That," Louisville Journal, sect. 3, p. 9, Jan. 11, 1920.

Aaron, Paul and Musto, David. "Temperance and Prohibition in America: A Historical Overview," ncbi.nlm.nih.gov.

"About Pig Stand & Staff," sanantoniopigstand.com, Jan. 29, 2014.

"About Us," The Berry Patch, worldslargeststrawberry.com.

"About Us," Casey's, caseys.com.

"Airstream: The 1930s," airstream.com/heritage.

"Alabama Products Lunch Slated Here Wednesday," Montgomery (Ala.) Advertiser, p. 8, April 22, 1970.

"Alamo Plaza Courts Hotel," wacohistory.org, cached Feb. 6, 2021.

"Alcohol," Maine An Encyclopedia, maineanencyclopedia.com.

"Announcing the Opening of Alamo Plaza" (ad), Tyler Courier-Times, p. 7, July 5, 1931.

"Asheville's Newest – Finest" (ad), Asheville Citizen-Times, p. K9, July 27, 1952.

"Auto-campers are welcome," The Orlando Sentinel (quoting the Jacksonville Observer), p. 2, Sept. 27, 1923.

"Automatic Signal System Approved," Chattanooga Daily Times, p. 5, Sept. 8, 1924.

Babson, Roger. "Mobile House Development Is Predicted," Arizona Republic, sect. 2, p. 1, Nov. 16, 1936.

Baker, Caitlin and Quillin, Martha. "Strawberry season ripens earlier," The Cary (N.C.) News, p. 3A, April 8, 2012.

Baker, Pamela L. "The Washington National Road Bill and the Struggle to Adopt a Federal System of Internal Improvement," Journal of the Early Republic, Vol. 22, No. 3, Autumn 2002.

Balusik, Chris. "Chrispie Crème a family's labor of love," chillicothegazette.com, Sept. 3, 2016.

"Barbecue." Columbia Missouri Herald, p. 3, Sept. 14, 1876.

"Barbecue Any Old Time," historysouth.org.

Barker, William J. "Motor Courts Out to Steal U.S. Tourists," Chicago Tribune, pt. 6, p. 6, June 6, 1948.

Barksdale, Nate. "How Drive-Thru Dining Changed Fast Food," history.com, "Beer would help dry enforcement, Andrews admits," Washington Evening Star, p. 1, April 14, 1926.

"The Berry Patch," visitnc.com.

Blount, Chuck. "San Antonio Pig Stand the last of its kind," expressnews.com, Dec. 6, 2017.

Bojangles.com.

Bovino, Arthur. "Sandwich of the Week: Dwarf House Chick-fil-A," thedailymeal.com, May 23, 2011.

"Bridge's Barbecue Lodge, Shelby," ncbbqsociety.com.

Broasted Chicken ad, Idaho State Journal, p. 33, Sept. 29, 1957.

Browne, Jeron. "Rooted in Slavery: Prison Labor Exploitation," reimagine.org.

Browne, Michael. "7-Eleven buying 3,900 Speedway stores in $21 billion deal," supermarketnews.com, Aug. 3, 2020.

Brownwell, Blaine A. "A Symbol of Modernity: Attitudes Toward the Automobile in Southern Cities in the 1920s," American Quarterly, Vol. 24, No. 1, pp. 20-44, March 1972.

Bruce, H. Addington. "Daniel Boone and the Wilderness Road," The Macmillan Company, New York, 1911.

"The Buffalo and New Orleans Road," editorial in the Raleigh Star, quoted in the North Carolina Free Press, p. 3, April 30, 1830.

Calise, Gabrielle. "'Highways of Hope': Read a Times reporter's account of a road trip through racism in 1964," Tampa Bay Times, tampabay.com, March 8, 2019.

Carfagno, Jacalyn. "Parkette Drive-In doing 'very good' despite pandemic," Lexington Herald-Leader, p. A1, May 18, 2020.

Carlitz, Ruth. "Hot Doughnuts Now: The Krispy Kreme Story," dukechronicle.com, Oct. 22, 2003.

Cathey, Dave. "80 years later, folks still line up for Van's Pig Stand," oklahoman.com, June 2, 2010.

"Changes in Agriculture, 1900 5o 1950," www2.census.gov.

Chertoff, Emily. "Cracker Barrel's Oddly Authentic Version of American History," theatlantic.com, March 2, 2013.

Cinematreasures.org.

"Circle K completes deal adding 435 stores in Southeast," Arizona Republic, p. E1, Oct. 6, 1984.

"Circle K founder Hervey dead at age 90," Tucson Citizen, p. 17, Sept. 7, 1999.

Clark, Walter. "The Colony of Transylvania," penelope.uchicago,edu.

"Congestion is a Handicap to Electric Rwy," Staunton (Va.) Evening Leader, p. 8, Feb. 22, 1925.

Conway, Hugh and Toth, James E. "Building Victory's Foundation: Infrastructure," American Logistics in World War II, ibiblio.org.

"Covered Bridge Manual," Federal Highway Administration, April 2005.

"Cuisine of the Southern United States facts for kids," kids.kiddle.co.

Dart, Bob. "Y'all amigos just come on down," Atlanta Constitution, p. 1H, Jan. 20, 1985.

"Delicious Krispy Kreme Donuts" (ad), Decatur (Ill.) Daily Review, p. 9, Nov. 9, 1935.

Dewey, Caitlin. "Advocates Rally to Tear Down Highways That Bulldozed Black Neighborhoods," pewtrusts.org, July 28, 2020.

Diamond, Rick and Moezzi, Mithra. "Changing Trends: A Brief History of the US Household Consumption of Energy, Water, Food, Beverages and Tobacco," homes.lbl.com.

"Dick's Drive-In," menupix.com.

"Don't Yell for Hercules If You're Stuck" (Piggly Wiggly ad), The Huntsville (Ala.) Times, p. 2, Feb. 11, 1923.

Downs, Jere. "Revival 'tarnishes' the icon," Louisville Courier-Journal, p. A1, May 28, 2015.

HIGHWAYS OF THE SOUTH

"Drive Negroes from Atlanta," Fort Worth Telegram, p. 1, Sept. 23, 1906.
"Drive-Ins all over the world," driveinmovie.com.
Dunn, Paul B. "A Stroll Through Fitzgerald, GA, In The Forties," Thomas Max Publishing, 2005.
Duvall, John S. "Military Construction at Home," ncpedia.org, spring 2008.
"Eggs brought $4 per dozen," Charlotte News, p. 3, Jan. 10, 1920.
Electric Lunch ad, Corvallis (Ore.) Gazette-Times, p. 4, May 14, 1953.
"Exploring the Oldest Road in The USA — The King's Highway," exploreglobalcreations.com.
Farfan, Barbara. "The World's Largest Convenience Store," thebalnacemb.com, Aug. 5, 2019.
Farrell, Sean. "Not Just Farms Anymore: The Effects of World War II on Mississippi's Economy," mshistorynow.mdah.state.ms.us.
Finch, Jackie. "Kentucky's doorway to the West," Martinsville (Ind.) Hoosier Times, p. H3, May 9, 2004.
"Fire Loss Put At $75,000," Atlanta Constitution, p. 9, Feb. 25, 1960.
"Franklin County Moonshine Stills," moonshineheritage.com, Feb. 28, 2012.
"From cell hear funeral service," Elizabeth City (N.C.) Daily Advance, p. 1, Aug. 12, 1921.
"Fuel efficiency of vehicles on the road: Little progress since the 1920s," news.umich.edu, May 5, 2009.
Fulton, Elissa. "Fill-Up with Billups," todayinmississippi.com.
"The Gospel Tent Revival," Memphis Avalanche, p. 1, May 20, 1885.
Grayburn, Kathryn. "Portraitist Returns from Paris To Present One-Man Show Here," Atlanta Constitution, p. 29, Sept. 15, 1961.
"The Greatest Generation," texastimetravel.com.
Harden, Mike. "Lesser-known Crispie Crème happy to stay in Chillicothe," Columbus Dispatch, Nov. 28, 2004.
"Has Man-Sized Drink For Every Male in United States," Topeka State Journal, p. 1, July 31, 1920.
Hayes, John. "Federal Road," georgiaencyclopedia.org, July 20, 2020.
Heitz, Kelly. "The Story of the Chicken Finger," southmag.com, April 1, 2016.
Hendricks, David. "Bill Church Jr. expanded Church's into an extensive fast-food chain," expressnews.com, Feb. 19, 2014.
Hicks, Nelson. "6 things you didn't know about the Big Chicken," wsbtv.com, June 29, 2018.
"Hidden History: Tuberculosis in Mammoth Cave," nps.gov.
Hill, H.J. "The History of Brush Arbors," theclasssroom.com, May 17, 2019.
Hilton, Matthew. "Cigarette Wars review," The Business History Review, Vol. 75, No. 2, Summer 2001.
Hinton, Ed. "Encore for a Fallen Lady," Atlanta Journal and Constitution, p, 14-D, July 15, 1979.
"Historic and Architectural Resources of Rockingham County, North Carolina, ca. 1799-1953, National Register of Historic Places Multiple Property Documentation Form, files.nc.gov, Oct. 14, 2003.
"Historic Bob White Covered Bridge destroyed in Patrick County flood,": wxii12.com, Sept. 30, 2015.
"The History of BBQ," bbq-my-way.com.
"History of Barbecuing," oscarenterprises.f2s.com.
"The History of Mobile Home Parks," mobilehomeuniversity.com.
"History of Moonshine and Prohibition in the United States South," oxfordtreatment.com, Oct. 8, 2020.
"A History of Moonshine Production in Franklin County, VA," fcdmoonshine.com.
"History of the Tennessee Highway Department," Nashville, Tennessee, tn.gov, 1959.
Hoekstra, Dave. "Living Color of the Mountaineer Inn," davehoekstra.com, July 21, 2015.
"The Holiday Inn Story," Indiana Evening Gazette, p. 22, April 23, 1965.
Horton, Caitlin L. "The Holiday Inn Great Sign," memphistypehistory.com, July 1, 2015.
"How Cars Became Dining Rooms: The History of Drive-Thrus," carrentals.com.
"Iconic Robert E. Lee Motel Demolished," heraldcourier.com, Oct. 12, 2009.
Isaacs, Barbara. "Poor Boy burgers and a rich tradition," Lexington Herald Leader, p. K1, March 22, 1992.
"Itinerant preacher convicted of bigamy," Bristol (Tenn.) Herald Courier.
"Itinerant Preacher Fired 14 Houses, Stepson's Claim After His Arrest," The Tennessean, p. 1, Sept. 21, 1927.

Jakle, John A. "The American Gasoline Station, 1920 to 1970," Journal of American Culture, Vol. 1, No. 3, Fall 1978.
Jakle, John A., and Sculle, Keith A. "The Gas Station in America," Johns Hopkins University Press, 1994.
Kazenski, Donna J. "Aimee Semple McPherson," historyswomen.com.
"The Kings Highway," carolana.com.
Klein, Daniel B., and Majewski, John. "Turnpikes and Toll Roads in Nineteenth-Century America," eh.net.
"Krispy Kreme Do-Nuts Made Every Two Hours," Asheville Citizen-Times, p. 5, March 7, 1938.
"Krispy Kreme Doughnuts, Inc. History," fundinguniverse.com.
"Krispy Kreme opens branch in W. Asheville," Asheville (N.C.) Times-Citizen, p. 5, Jan. 31, 1938.
"Krystal Burger Headquarters & History," burgerbeast.com, June 7, 2017 / updated Nov. 24, 2020.
"Krystal hamburgers a Southern tradition," Greenwood (S.C.) Index-Journal, pl 18, Dec. 30, 1983.
"'The Krystal' Opens," Chattanooga News, "p. 9, Oct. 25, 1932.
"Krystal: The History of Hamburger Restaurant Chains," restaurantnews.com, May 4, 2011.
Lacey-Bordeaux, Emma and Drash, Wayne. "Travel guide helped African-Americans navigate tricky times," edition.cnn.com, Feb. 25, 2011.
Lammle, Rob. "11 Facts about 7-Eleven on 7/11," mentalfloss.com, July 11, 2018.
Lammle, Rob. "The Cool History of the Slurpee," mentalfloss.com, Nov. 15, 2010.
Lauderdale, Vance. "Remembering the Alamo — Plaza, That Is," memphisflyer.com, Dec. 1, 2008.
Leonard, Edmund P. "State Gasoline Taxes," Bulletin of the University of Kansas Humanistic Studies, March 15, 1925.
"Legal Notices," Newport News Daily Press, p. 14, Jan. 28, 1957.
Lichtenstein, Alex. "Forced Labor and Progress," versobooks.com, Feb. 26, 2017.
Litsch, Joseph. "From A Dwarf To A Giant," Atlanta Constitution, p. 1-B, Nov. 15, 1979.
Little, Becky. "How Prohibition Fueled the Rise of the Ku Klux Klan," history.com, Jan. 15, 2019.
"Lloyd A. Renison," Asheville Citizen-Times, p. 13, Jan. 12, 1985.
"Looking Back at Year-End School Traditions," Museum & Archives of Rockingham County, themarconline.org, May 15, 2020.
Luna, Melinda. "The Waco Traffic Circle: An Early Texas Roundabout," texasce.org.
Madden, Bridget. "July 1937: Krispy Kreme Opens in Winston-Salem," blogs.lib.unc.edu, July 1, 2009.
Mallon, Paul R. "Greater Part of Dixie Highway From Louisville To Mammoth Cave As Smooth As Bald Head," Louisville Courier-Journal, p.35, July 27, 1919.
"Mammoth Cave National Park," ohranger.com.
"Markers memorialize evangelist," Marshal (Texas) News Messenger, p. 6A, April 10, 2010.
Markovich, Jeremy. "The History of Family Dollar Stores," ourstate.com, July 31, 2013.
Martin, Douglas. "Al Copeland, a Restaurateur Known for Spice and Speed, Dies at 64," nytimes.com, March 25, 2008.
Martin, Stump. "Historic Roy's Grill Opens In Rossville," chattanoogan.com, Jan. 24, 2011.
Maze, Jonathan. "Cracker Barrel, Kraft Settle Differences," Restaurant Finance Monitor, restfinance.com, Oct. 4, 2013.
McCartney, Keeler. "5 Labor Day Lakewood Auto Racers Possess Lengthy Police Records," Atlanta Constitution, p. 1, Aug. 31, 1945.
"Missouri Drive-ins," roadarch.com.
Miyano, Miran. "KFC Just Dropped Its Iconic 'It's Finger Lickin' Good' Tagline Due to COVID-19," vice.com, Aug. 26, 2020.
Moody, John. "The Railroad Builders: A Chronicle of the Welding of the States," Yale University Press, 1919.
"Moonshine raids in Kentucky bloodless," Winston-Salem Journal, p. 7, Dec. 25, 1920.
Morris, Regan. "A postman wrote a Route 66 travel guide for black people," bbc.com, Dec. 23, 2016.
Morrison, Jim. "Commemorating 100 Years of the RV," Smithsonian Magazine, smiosonianmag.org, Aug. 24, 2010.
Mossman, Matt. "Smithsonian exhibit extolls South's beloved doughnut," Morristown (N.J.) Daily Record, p. A10, July 18, 1997.
"'Natural Bridge' by Paul McGehee," paulmcgeheeart.com.
"New do-nuts are popular," Charlotte Observer, sect. 4, p. 19, March 20, 1938.
"New entrance to Mammoth hit by action," Louisville Courier-Journal, p. 1, Aug. 25, 1926.

HIGHWAYS OF THE SOUTH

New Tourist Apartments Filling Fast," Tyler (Texas) Morning Telegraph, p. 10, July 2, 1931.
O'Brien Wagner, Nancy. "*Slavery by Another Name* History Background," bento.cdn.pbs.org.
Oh, Soo. "Which states count as the South, according to more than 40,000 readers," vox.com, Sept. 30, 2016.
Okrent, Daniel. "Wayne B. Wheeler: The Man Who Turned Off the Taps," smithsonianmag.com, May 2020.
"Old King's Highway," scpictureproject.org.
Pauls, Elizabeth Prine. "Trail of Tears," brittanica.com.
Pierce, John R. "The Fuel Consumption of Automobiles," Scientific American, Vol. 232, No. 1, Jan. 1975.
"Proper Regulation of Tourist Cabins," The Capital Times (Madison, Wis.), p. 16, Jan. 29, 1940.
Provost, Stephen H. "Martinsville Memories," Dragon Crown Books, 2019.
"R.D. Bond Tire & Supply Co." (ad), Knoxville Sentinel, p. 12, Jan. 10, 1920.
"Regulations for Tourist Camps," The Capital Times (Madison, Wis.), p. 16, Jan. 29, 1940.
"Regulation of Tourist Camps," The Wilkes-Barre Record, p. 14, March 13, 1940.
"Reidsville," The Danville Bee, p. 2, Jan. 27, 1954.
"Religious Landscape Study," Pew Research Center, pewforum.org, 2015.
"The Remnants of Prohibition," prohibition.themobmuseum.org.
"Restaurants vote to end price cuts," Chattanooga Times, p. 9, Feb. 8, 1934.
"Rev. Sam Jones..." Anderson (S.C.) Intelligencer, p. 2, June 4, 1885.
Ricke, Temple. "Way Back Wednesday: The King's Highway," counton2.com, April 20, 2020.
"Rich History Of Winston-Salem, NC," winston-salemdentists.com.
"Roadside Architecture of Kentucky's Dixie Highways," heritage.ky.gov, Oct. 1, 2004.
"Roadside Communities: Rin's Rest, Muirkirk, Maryland," americanhistory.si.edu.
Ruscin, Terry. "Beyond the Banks: The Gospel of Good Roads," blueridgenow.com, March 11, 2018.
"Sales and leases are more active," Atlanta Constitution, p. 5B, Jan. 16, 1938.
Sanders, Colonel Harland. "The Autobiography of the Original Celebrity Chef," KFC Corporation, Louisville, Ky., 2012.
Scavotto, Andrew. "Dollar General Founder Cal Turner Sr. Loved Small Town Life," nashvillepost.com.
Schremp Hahn, Valerie. "Something is going on in Uranus," Minneapolis Star-Tribune, p. G6, Jan. 21, 2018.
Scott, John W. "Highway Building in Louisiana Before Huey Long: An Overdue Re-Appraisal," Louisiana History: The Journal of the Louisiana Historical Association, Vol. 44, No. 1, Winter 2003.
"Selling Entrance To Kentucky Caves," Carbondale (Ill.) Free Press, p. 2, Sept. 5, 1922.
Sherman, Chris. "Neighborly Toddle House Coming to Town," Orlando Sentinel, orlandosentinel.com, Jan. 11, 1987.
Sismondo, Christine. "What Prohibition teaches us about race relations in the U.S.," macleans.ca, June 11, 2020.
Smith, John M. "A visit to the 'Moonshine Capital of the World," Central Hastings News, issuu.com, March 26, 2015.
Smith, Robert J. "Natural Bridge of Virginia," cei.org, June 1, 1998.
Smith, Tim. "How South Carolina came to own so many roads," Greenville News, greenvilleonline.com, April 3, 2017.
"Snowbound Tourists Flock Pulaski, Columbia Hotels," Nashville Tennessean, p. 40, Jan, 30, 1948.
Sorenson, Karen. "Faith: The Rise and fall of tent revival church services," tauntongazette.com, June 16, 2010.
"South Of The Border," roadsideamerica.com.
Start, Clarissa. "Big Shot at 40 With Mama's Help," St. Louis Post-Dispatch, p. 3F, Aug. 2, 1953.
"State Motor Vehicle Registrations, By Years, 1900-1995," fhwa.dot.gov.
Stice, Joel. "The Untold Truth Of Church's Chicken," mashed.com, June 5, 2020.
"South Carolina Historic Properties Record," schpr.cs.gov.
Sutton, Amber. "12 things you might not know about Krystal," al.com, April 12, 2016 / updated May 18, 2019.
Tabler, Dave. "America's Roadside Evangelist," appalachianhistory.net, Aug. 24, 2017.
Tabler, Dave. "That old-time tent revival," appalachianhistory.net, July 18, 2919.
Tabler, Dave. "We cannot believe Christ would use tobacco in any form," appalachianhistory.net, Jan. 31, 2019.
"Tanner's Big Orange: Serving Greenville for over 75 years," tannersbigorange.com.

Taube, David. "Here are the most, least restrictive fireworks laws by state," wmur.com, July 4, 2017.

Taylor, Kate. "7 Things You Didn't Know About the Real Colonel Sanders," entrepreneur.com, Sept. 4, 2015.

Tennis, Joe. "Col. Sanders Once Cooked At Lee Motel," heraldcourier.com, July 19, 2008.

"Tent Revival Meetings Will Continue," Los Angeles Evening Citizen, p. 2, Oct. 24, 1949.

"Tent Revival to Close With Famous Sermon," Los Angeles Times, part II, p. 3, Nov. 12, 1949.

Tiede, Tom. "'Get Right with God,' Says Henry Harrison Mayes," Marysville (Mo.) Daily Forum, p. 2, Jan. 6, 1975.

"Trail of Tears," history.com, Nov. 9, 2009 / updated July 7, 2020.

Trailers and trailer camps in the community," American Society of Planning Officials, Information Report No. 12, March 1950.

Truman, Cheryl. "Iconic Burger Shake sign awaits new numbers as burger price hits three figures," kentucky.com, Nov. 6, 2014.

Turner, Walter R. "Transportation Improvements in the 1920s," Tar Heel Junior Historian Association, ncpedia.org, 2004.

"Uranus," visitmo.com.

Vaughn, Daniel. "The History of the Pig Stands," texasmonthly.com, Feb. 18, 2015.

"Valley Turnpike," virginiaplaces.org.

"Waffle House didn't cook up an empire overnight," Atlanta Journal-Constitution, p. E9, Aug. 18, 2019.

"The Waffle House," Northumberland (Pa.) Public Press, p. 3, Jan. 18, 1884.

Warnick, Ron. "Boots Court in Carthage officially put up for sale," route66news.com, May 14, 2020.

Weingroff, Richard F. "The Greatest Decade 1956-1966: Part 2 The Battle of Its Life," fhwa.dot.gov.

Weingroff, Richard F. "The Lincoln Highway," fhwa.dog.gov.

"What to Eat," Harrisburg Star-Independent, p. 9, May 22, 1903.

"What's happening to bowling?" whitehutchinson.com.

Wiersema, Libby. "South Carolina's South of the Border survives modern times," greensboro.com, July 18, 2017.

"Wilderness Road," history.com, Aug. 21, 2018.

"Wiley L. Moore — Citizen of Georgia," Pure Oil News, April 1945.

Winnerman, Jim. "Rabid collectors spawn small museums to house their treasures," St. Louis Post-Dispatch, p. T1, Dec. 29, 2002.

"Wintry winds drive many to Hotel de Jail," Knoxville News-Sentinel, p. 15, Nov. 21, 1929.

Whitaker, Beverly. "The Great Valley Road," freepages.rootsweb.com.

"Why are Covered Bridges Covered?" study.com.

Woco Pep ad, "Simpson County (Miss.) News, p. 6, May 9, 1929.

"Woman evangelist is coming in auto to show you the way to heaven," St. Louis Post-Dispatch Sunday Magazine, p. 13, Aug. 24, 1919.

"Women Led the Temperance Charge," prohibition.themobmuseum.org.

"Wood County Students Win Prizes In Essay Contest," Wisconsin Rapids Daily Tribune, p. 6, May 20, 1924.

"World Records," buc-ees.com.

Wyatt, Kristen. "Waffle House still dishin' diner food at 50," nbcnews.com, April 15, 2005.

Young, Terence. "A Brief History of the RV," Smithsonian Magazine, smithsonianmag.com, Sept. 4, 2018.

Photo by Samaire Provost

About the author

Stephen H. Provost has written several books about life in 20th century America. This is his fifth book on America's highways and third in the *America's Historic Highways* series. During more than three decades in journalism, he has worked as a managing editor, copy desk chief, columnist and reporter at five newspapers. Now a full-time author, he has written on such diverse topics as dragons, mutant superheroes, mythic archetypes, language, department stores and his hometown. He currently lives in Martinsville. Visit him online and read his blogs at stephenhprovost.com.

Did you enjoy this book?

Recommend it to a friend. And please consider rating it and/or leaving a brief review online at Amazon, Barnes & Noble and Goodreads.

Also by the author

Works of Fiction

The Talismans of Time (Academy of the Lost Labyrinth, Book 1)

Pathfinder of Destiny (Academy of the Lost Labyrinth, Book 2)

Astral Academy

Memortality (The Memortality Saga, Book 1)

Paralucidity (The Memortality Saga, Book 2)

The Only Dragon

Identity Break

Feathercap

Nightmare's Eve

Works of Nonfiction

Yesterday's Highways

America's First Highways

Highway 99: The History of California's Main Street

Highway 101: The History of El Camino Real

The Great American Shopping Experience

Martinsville Memories

Fresno Growing Up

A Whole Different League

The Legend of Molly Bolin

Please Stop Saying That!

50 Undefeated

Media Meltdown

Political Psychosis

Jesus, You're Fired!

The Phoenix Chronicles (3 books)

The Phoenix Principle (2 books)

Praise for other works

"If you have any interest in highways, old diners and motels and such, or 20th century US history, this book is for you. It is without a doubt one of the best highway books ever published."
— Dan R. Young, founder OLD HIGHWAY 101 group, on **Yesterday's Highways**

"Both books are well-researched, nicely written, and illustrated with good black and white photographs, and both contribute importantly to highway literature."
— Wayne Shannon, *Jefferson Highway Declaration*, on **Yesterday's Highways** and **America's First Highways**

"... an engaging narrative that pulls the reader into the story and onto the road. ... I highly recommend **Highway 99: The History of California's Main Street**, whether you're a roadside archaeology nut or just someone who enjoys a ripping story peppered with vintage photographs."
— Barbara Gossett, Society for Commercial Archaeology Journal

"Profusely illustrated throughout, **Highway 99** is unreservedly recommended as an essential and core addition to every community and academic library's California History collections."
— California Bookwatch

"... it contains a lot of information I hadn't heard before. Both books prove well-written with few weaknesses..."
— Ron Warnick, route66news.com, on **Yesterday's Highways** and **America's First Highways**

"An essential primer for anyone seeking an entrée into the genre. Provost serves up a smorgasbord of highlights gleaned from his personal memories of and research into the various nooks and crannies of what 'used-to-be' in professional team sports."
— Tim Hanlon, Good Seats Still Available, on **A Whole Different League**

"As informed and informative as it is entertaining and absorbing, **Fresno Growing Up** is very highly recommended for personal, community, and academic library 20th Century American History collections."

— John Burroughs, Reviewer's Bookwatch

"The complex idea of mixing morality and mortality is a fresh twist on the human condition. ... **Memortality** is one of those books that will incite more questions than it answers. And for fandom, that's a good thing."

— Ricky L. Brown, Amazing Stories

"Punchy and fast paced, **Memortality** reads like a graphic novel. ... (Provost's) style makes the trippy landscapes and mind-bending plot points more believable and adds a thrilling edge to this vivid crossover fantasy."

— Foreword Reviews

"The genres in this volume span horror, fantasy, and science-fiction, and each is handled deftly. ... **Nightmare's Eve** should be on your reading list. The stories are at the intersection of nightmare and lucid dreaming, up ahead a signpost ... next stop, your reading pile. Keep the nightlight on."

— R.B. Payne, Cemetery Dance

"**Memortality** by Stephen Provost is a highly original, thrilling novel unlike anything else out there."

— David McAfee, bestselling author of *33 A.D., 61 A.D.,* and *79 A.D.*

"Provost sticks mostly to the classics: vampires, ghosts, aliens, and even dragons. But trekking familiar terrain allows the author to subvert readers' expectations. ... Provost's poetry skillfully displays the same somber themes as the stories. ... Worthy tales that prove external forces are no more terrifying than what's inside people's heads."

— Kirkus Reviews on **Nightmare's Eve**

"The story feels so close, so intimate, we as readers experience the emotions, the events, and the conflicts, in what feels like real time. Gut-wrenchingly so."

— Stephen Mark Rainey, author of *Blue Devil Island*, on **Death's Doorstep**

www.ingramcontent.com/pod-product-compliance
Lightning Source LLC
Chambersburg PA
CBHW081915170426
43200CB00014B/2731